ON THE MAKING OF MAN

SAINT GREGORY OF NYSSA

AETERNA PRESS

PUBLISHED BY AETERNA PRESS.
COVER DESIGN BY AETERNA PRESS.

DOGMATIC TREATISES, ETC. CREATOR(S): GREGORY OF NYSSA SCHAFF, PHILIP (1819–1893) (EDITOR) PRINT BASIS: NEW YORK: CHRISTIAN LITERATURE PUBLISHING CO., 1892.

ISBN-13: 978-1-78516-880-2

AVAILABLE AS AN E-BOOK:
WWW.AETERNAPRESS.COM

CONTENTS

INTRODUCTION 1

I. WHEREIN IS A PARTIAL INQUIRY INTO THE NATURE OF THE WORLD, AND A MORE MINUTE EXPOSITION OF THE THINGS WHICH PRECEDED THE GENESIS OF MAN 5

II. WHY MAN APPEARED LAST, AFTER THE CREATION 7

III. THAT THE NATURE OF MAN IS MORE PRECIOUS THAN ALL THE VISIBLE CREATION 8

IV. THAT THE CONSTRUCTION OF MAN THROUGHOUT SIGNIFIES HIS RULING POWER 9

V. THAT MAN IS A LIKENESS OF THE DIVINE SOVEREIGNTY 9

VI. AN EXAMINATION OF THE KINDRED OF MIND TO NATURE: WHEREIN, BY WAY OF DIGRESSION, IS REFUTED THE DOCTRINE OF THE ANOMOEANS 10

VII. WHY MAN IS DESTITUTE OF NATURAL WEAPONS AND COVERING 11

VIII. WHY MAN'S FORM IS UPRIGHT; AND THAT HANDS WERE GIVEN HIM BECAUSE OF REASON; WHEREIN ALSO IS A SPECULATION ON THE DIFFERENCE OF SOULS 13

IX. THAT THE FORM OF MAN WAS FRAMED TO SERVE AS AN INSTRUMENT FOR THE USE OF REASON 16

X. THAT THE MIND WORKS BY MEANS OF THE SENSES 17

XI. THAT THE NATURE OF MIND IS INVISIBLE 19

XII. AN EXAMINATION OF THE QUESTION WHERE THE RULING PRINCIPLE IS TO BE CONSIDERED TO RESIDE; WHEREIN ALSO IS A DISCUSSION OF TEARS AND LAUGHTER, AND A PHYSIOLOGICAL SPECULATION AS TO THE INTER-RELATION OF MATTER, NATURE, AND MIND 20

XIII. A RATIONALE OF SLEEP, OF YAWNING, AND OF DREAMS 25

XIV. THAT THE MIND IS NOT IN A PART OF THE BODY; WHEREIN ALSO IS A DISTINCTION OF THE MOVEMENTS OF THE BODY AND OF THE SOUL 30

XV. THAT THE SOUL PROPER, IN FACT AND NAME, IS THE RATIONAL SOUL, WHILE THE OTHERS ARE CALLED SO EQUIVOCALLY; WHEREIN ALSO IS THIS STATEMENT, THAT THE POWER OF THE MIND EXTENDS THROUGHOUT THE WHOLE BODY IN FITTING CONTACT WITH EVERY PART 31

XVI. A CONTEMPLATION OF THE DIVINE UTTERANCE WHICH SAID—"LET US MAKE MAN AFTER OUR IMAGE AND LIKENESS"; WHEREIN IS EXAMINED WHAT IS THE DEFINITION OF THE IMAGE, AND HOW THE PASSIBLE AND MORTAL IS LIKE TO THE BLESSED AND IMPASSIBLE, AND HOW IN THE IMAGE THERE ARE MALE AND FEMALE, SEEING THESE ARE NOT IN THE PROTOTYPE 32

XVII. WHAT WE MUST ANSWER TO THOSE WHO RAISE THE QUESTION—"IF PROCREATION IS AFTER SIN, HOW WOULD SOULS HAVE COME INTO BEING IF THE FIRST OF MANKIND HAD REMAINED SINLESS ?" 37

XVIII. THAT OUR IRRATIONAL PASSIONS HAVE THEIR RISE FROM KINDRED WITH IRRATIONAL NATURE 39

XIX. TO THOSE WHO SAY THAT THE ENJOYMENT OF THE GOOD THINGS WE LOOK FOR WILL AGAIN CONSIST IN MEAT AND DRINK, BECAUSE IT IS WRITTEN THAT BY THESE MEANS MAN AT FIRST LIVED IN PARADISE 41

XX. WHAT WAS THE LIFE IN PARADISE, AND WHAT WAS THE FORBIDDEN TREE ? 42

XXI. THAT THE RESURRECTION IS LOOKED FOR AS A CONSEQUENCE, NOT SO MUCH FROM THE DECLARATION OF SCRIPTURE AS FROM THE VERY NECESSITY OF THINGS 44

XXII. TO THOSE WHO SAY, "IF THE RESURRECTION IS A THING EXCELLENT AND GOOD, HOW IS IT THAT IT HAS NOT HAPPENED ALREADY, BUT IS HOPED FOR IN SOME PERIODS OF TIME?" 45

XXIII. THAT HE WHO CONFESSES THE BEGINNING OF THE WORLD'S EXISTENCE MUST NECESSARILY ALSO AGREE AS TO ITS END 48

XXIV. AN ARGUMENT AGAINST THOSE WHO SAY THAT MATTER IS CO-ETERNAL WITH GOD 50

XXV. HOW ONE EVEN OF THOSE WHO ARE WITHOUT MAY BE BROUGHT TO BELIEVE THE SCRIPTURE WHEN TEACHING OF THE RESURRECTION 51

XXVI. THAT THE RESURRECTION IS NOT BEYOND PROBABILITY 56

XXVII. THAT IT IS POSSIBLE, WHEN THE HUMAN BODY IS DISSOLVED INTO THE ELEMENTS OF THE UNIVERSE, THAT EACH SHOULD HAVE HIS OWN BODY RESTORED FROM THE COMMON SOURCE 57

XXVIII. TO THOSE WHO SAY THAT SOULS EXISTED BEFORE BODIES, OR THAT BODIES WERE FORMED BEFORE SOULS; WHEREIN THERE IS ALSO A REFUTATION OF THE FABLES CONCERNING TRANSMIGRATION OF SOULS 59

XXIX. AN ESTABLISHMENT OF THE DOCTRINE THAT THE CAUSE OF THE EXISTENCE OF SOUL AND BODY IS ONE AND THE SAME 62

XXX. A BRIEF EXAMINATION OF THE CONSTRUCTION OF OUR BODIES FROM A MEDICAL POINT OF VIEW 65

INTRODUCTION

Gregory, Bishop of Nyssa, to his brother Peter, the servant of God.

If we had to honour with rewards of money those who excel in virtue, the whole world of money, as Solomon says , would seem but small to be made equal to your virtue in the balance. Since, however, the debt of gratitude due to your Reverence is greater than can be valued in money, and the holy Eastertide demands the accustomed gift of love, we offer to your greatness of mind, O man of God, a gift too small indeed to be worthy of presentation to you, yet not falling short of the extent of our power. The gift is a discourse, like a mean garment, woven not without toil from our poor wit, and the subject of the discourse, while it will perhaps be generally thought audacious, yet seemed not unfitting. For he alone has worthily considered the creation of God who truly was created after God, and whose soul was fashioned in the image of Him Who created him,—Basil, our common father and teacher,—who by his own speculation made the sublime ordering of the universe generally intelligible, making the world as established by God in the true Wisdom known to those who by means of his understanding are led to such contemplation: but we, who fall short even of worthily admiring him, yet intend to add to the great writer's speculations that which is lacking in them, not so as to interpolate his work by insertion (for it is not to be thought of that that lofty mouth should suffer the insult of being given as authority for our discourses), but so that the glory of the teacher may not seem to be failing among his disciples.

For if, the consideration of man being lacking in his Hexaemeron, none of those who had been his disciples contributed any earnest effort to supply the defect, the scoffer would perhaps have had a handle against his great fame, on the ground that he had not cared to produce in his hearers any habit of intelligence. But now that we venture according to our powers upon the exposition of what was lacking, if anything should be found in our work such as to be not unworthy of his teaching, it will surely be referred to our teacher: while if our discourse does not reach the height of his sublime speculation, he will be free from this charge and escape the blame of seeming not to wish that his disciples should have any skill at all, though we perhaps may be answerable to our censurers as being unable to contain in the littleness of our heart the wisdom of our instructor.

The scope of our proposed enquiry is not small: it is second to none of the wonders of the world,—perhaps even greater than any of those known to us, because no other existing thing, save the human creation, has been made like to God: thus we shall readily find that allowance will be made for what we say by kindly readers, even if our discourse is far behind the merits of the subject. For it is our business, I suppose, to leave nothing unexamined of all that concerns man,—of what we believe to have taken place previously, of what we now see, and of the results which are expected afterwards to appear (for surely our effort would be convicted of failing of its promise, if, when man is proposed for contemplation, any of the questions which bear upon the subject were to be omitted); and, moreover, we must fit together, according to the explanation of Scripture and to that derived from reasoning, those statements concerning him which seem, by a kind of necessary sequence, to be opposed, so that our whole subject may be consistent in train of thought and in order, as the statements that seem to be contrary are brought (if the Divine power so discovers a hope for what is beyond hope, and a way for what is inextricable) to one and the same end: and for clearness' sake I think it well to set forth to you the discourse by chapters, that you may be able briefly to know the force of the several arguments of the whole work.

1. Wherein is a partial inquiry into the nature of the world, and a more minute exposition of the things which preceded the genesis of man.

2. Why man appeared last, after the creation.

3. That the nature of man is more precious than all the visible creation.

4. That the construction of man throughout signifies his ruling power.

5. That man is a likeness of the Divine sovereignty.

6. An examination of the kindred of mind to nature: wherein by way of digression is refuted the doctrine of the Anomoeans.

7. Why man is destitute of natural weapons and covering.

8. Why man's form is upright, and that hands were given him because of reason; wherein also is a speculation on the difference of souls.

9. That the form of man was framed to serve as an instrument for the use of reason.

10. That the mind works by means of the senses.

11. That the nature of mind is invisible.

12. An examination of the question where the ruling principle is to be considered to reside; wherein also is a discussion of tears and laughter, and a physiological speculation as to the interrelation of matter, nature, and mind.

13. A rationale of sleep, of yawning, and of dreams.

14. That the mind is not in a part of the body; wherein also is a distinction of the movements of the body and of the soul.

15. That the soul proper, in fact and name, is the rational soul, while the others are called so equivocally: wherein also is this statement, that the power of the mind extends throughout the whole body in fitting contact with every part.

16. A contemplation of the Divine utterance which said,—"Let us make man after our image and likeness;" wherein is examined what is the definition of the image, and how the passible and mortal is like to the Blessed and Impassible, and how in the image there are male and female, seeing these are not in the Prototype.

17. What we must answer to those who raise the question—"If procreation is after sin, how would souls have come into being if the first of mankind had remained sinless?"

18. That our irrational passions have their rise from kindred with irrational nature.

19. To those who say that the enjoyment of the good things we look for will again consist in meat and drink, because it is written that by these means man at first lived in Paradise.

20. What was the life in Paradise, and what was the forbidden tree.

21. That the resurrection is looked for as a consequence, not so much from the declaration of Scripture as from the very necessity of things.

22. To those who say, "If the resurrection is a thing excellent and good, how is it that it has not happened already, but is hoped for in some periods of time?"

23. That he who confesses the beginning of the world's existence must necessarily agree also as to its end.

24. An argument against those who say that matter is co-eternal with God.

25. How one even of those who are without may be brought to believe the Scripture when teaching of the resurrection.

26. That the resurrection is not beyond probability.

27. That it is possible, when the human body is dissolved into the elements of the universe, that each should have his own body restored from the common source.

28. To those who say that souls existed before bodies, or that bodies were formed before souls: wherein there is also a refutation of the fables concerning transmigrations of souls.

29. An establishment of the doctrine that the cause of existence of soul and body is one and the same.

30. A brief consideration of the construction of our bodies from a medical point of view.

I. WHEREIN IS A PARTIAL INQUIRY INTO THE NATURE OF THE WORLD, AND A MORE MINUTE EXPOSITION OF THE THINGS WHICH PRECEDED THE GENESIS OF MAN

1. "This is the book of the generation of heaven and earth ," saith the Scripture, when all that is seen was finished, and each of the things that are betook itself to its own separate place, when the body of heaven compassed all things round, and those bodies which are heavy and of downward tendency, the earth and the water, holding each other in, took the middle place of the universe; while, as a sort of bond and stability for the things that were made, the Divine power and skill was implanted in the growth of things, guiding all things with the reins of a double operation (for it was by rest and motion that it devised the genesis of the things that were not, and the continuance of the things that are), driving around, about the heavy and changeless element contributed by the creation that does not move, as about some fixed path, the exceedingly rapid motion of the sphere, like a wheel, and preserving the indissolubility of both by their mutual action, as the circling substance by its rapid motion compresses the compact body of the earth round about, while that which is firm and unyielding, by reason of its unchanging fixedness, continually augments the whirling motion of those things which revolve round it, and intensity is produced in equal measure in each of the natures which thus differ in their operation, in the stationary nature, I mean, and in the mobile revolution; for neither is the earth shifted from its own base, nor does the heaven ever relax in its vehemence, or slacken its motion.

2. These, moreover, were first framed before other things, according to the Divine wisdom, to be as it were a beginning of the whole machine, the great Moses indicating, I suppose, where he says that the heaven and the earth were made by God "in the beginning " that all things that are seen in the creation are the offspring of rest and motion, brought into being by the Divine will. Now the heaven and the earth being diametrically opposed to each other in their operations, the creation which lies between the opposites, and has in part a share in what is adjacent to it, itself acts as a mean between the extremes, so that there is manifestly a mutual contact of the opposites through the mean; for air in a manner imitates the perpetual motion and subtlety of the fiery substance, both in the lightness of its nature, and in its suitableness for motion; yet it is not such as to be alienated from the solid substance, for it is no more

in a state of continual flux and dispersion than in a permanent state of immobility, but becomes, in its affinity to each, a kind of borderland of the opposition between operations, at once uniting in itself and dividing things which are naturally distinct.

3. In the same way, liquid substance also is attached by double qualities to each of the opposites; for in so far as it is heavy and of downward tendency it is closely akin to the earthy; but in so far as it partakes of a certain fluid and mobile energy it is not altogether alien from the nature which is in motion; and by means of this also there is effected a kind of mixture and concurrence of the opposites, weight being transferred to motion, and motion finding no hindrance in weight, so that things most extremely opposite in nature combine with one another, and are mutually joined by those which act as means between them.

4. But to speak strictly, one should rather say that the very nature of the contraries themselves is not entirely without mixture of properties, each with the other, so that, as I think, all that we see in the world mutually agree, and the creation, though discovered in properties of contrary natures, is yet at union with itself. For as motion is not conceived merely as local shifting, but is also contemplated in change and alteration, and on the other hand the immovable nature does not admit motion by way of alteration, the wisdom of God has transposed these properties, and wrought unchangeableness in that which is ever moving, and change in that which is immovable; doing this, it may be, by a providential dispensation, so that that property of nature which constitutes its immutability and immobility might not, when viewed in any created object, cause the creature to be accounted as God; for that which may happen to move or change would cease to admit of the conception of Godhead. Hence the earth is stable without being immutable, while the heaven, on the contrary, as it has no mutability, so has not stability either, that the Divine power, by interweaving change in the stable nature and motion with that which is not subject to change, might, by the interchange of attributes, at once join them both closely to each other, and make them alien from the conception of Deity; for as has been said, neither of these (neither that which is unstable, nor that which is mutable) can be considered to belong to the more Divine nature.

5. Now all things were already arrived at their own end: "the heaven and the earth ," as Moses says, "were finished," and all things that lie between them, and the particular things were adorned with their appropriate beauty; the heaven with the rays of the stars, the sea and air with the living creatures that swim and fly, and the earth with all varieties of plants and animals, to all which, empowered by the Divine will, it gave birth together; the earth was full,

too, of her produce, bringing forth fruits at the same time with flowers; the meadows were full of all that grows therein, and all the mountain ridges, and summits, and every hillside, and slope, and hollow, were crowned with young grass, and with the varied produce of the trees, just risen from the ground, yet shot up at once into their perfect beauty; and all the beasts that had come into life at God's command were rejoicing, we may suppose, and skipping about, running to and fro in the thickets in herds according to their kind, while every sheltered and shady spot was ringing with the chants of the songbirds. And at sea, we may suppose, the sight to be seen was of the like kind, as it had just settled to quiet and calm in the gathering together of its depths, where havens and harbours spontaneously hollowed out on the coasts made the sea reconciled with the land; and the gentle motion of the waves vied in beauty with the meadows, rippling delicately with light and harmless breezes that skimmed the surface; and all the wealth of creation by land and sea was ready, and none was there to share it.

II. WHY MAN APPEARED LAST, AFTER THE CREATION

1. For not as yet had that great and precious thing, man, come into the world of being; it was not to be looked for that the ruler should appear before the subjects of his rule; but when his dominion was prepared, the next step was that the king should be manifested. When, then, the Maker of all had prepared beforehand, as it were, a royal lodging for the future king (and this was the land, and islands, and sea, and the heaven arching like a roof over them), and when all kinds of wealth had been stored in this palace (and by wealth I mean the whole creation, all that is in plants and trees, and all that has sense, and breath, and life; and—if we are to account materials also as wealth—all that for their beauty are reckoned precious in the eyes of men, as gold and silver, and the substances of your jewels which men delight in—having concealed, I say, abundance of all these also in the bosom of the earth as in a royal treasure-house), he thus manifests man in the world, to be the beholder of some of the wonders therein, and the lord of others; that by his enjoyment he might have knowledge of the Giver, and by the beauty and majesty of the things he saw might trace out that power of the Maker which is beyond speech and language.

2. For this reason man was brought into the world last after the creation, not being rejected to the last as worthless, but as one whom it behoved to be king over his subjects at his very birth. And as a good host does not bring his guest to his house before the preparation of his feast, but, when he has made all due preparation, and decked with their proper adornments his house, his

couches, his table, brings his guest home when things suitable for his refreshment are in readiness,—in the same manner the rich and munificent Entertainer of our nature, when He had decked the habitation with beauties of every kind, and prepared this great and varied banquet, then introduced man, assigning to him as his task not the acquiring of what was not there, but the enjoyment of the things which were there; and for this reason He gives him as foundations the instincts of a twofold organization, blending the Divine with the earthy, that by means of both he may be naturally and properly disposed to each enjoyment, enjoying God by means of his more divine nature, and the good things of earth by the sense that is akin to them.

III. THAT THE NATURE OF MAN IS MORE PRECIOUS THAN ALL THE VISIBLE CREATION

1. But it is right that we should not leave this point without consideration, that while the world, great as it is, and its parts, are laid as an elemental foundation for the formation of the universe, the creation is, so to say, made offhand by the Divine power, existing at once on His command, while counsel precedes the making of man; and that which is to be is foreshown by the Maker in verbal description, and of what kind it is fitting that it should be, and to what archetype it is fitting that it should bear a likeness, and for what it shall be made, and what its operation shall be when it is made, and of what it shall be the ruler,—all these things the saying examines beforehand, so that he has a rank assigned him before his genesis, and possesses rule over the things that are before his coming into being; for it says, "God said, Let us make man in our image, after our likeness, and let them have dominion over the fish of the sea, and the beasts of the earth, and the fowls of the heaven, and the cattle, and all the earth ."

2. O marvellous! a sun is made, and no counsel precedes; a heaven likewise; and to these no single thing in creation is equal. So great a wonder is formed by a word alone, and the saying indicates neither when, nor how, nor any such detail. So too in all particular cases, the aether, the stars, the intermediate air, the sea, the earth, the animals, the plants,—all are brought into being with a word, while only to the making of man does the Maker of all draw near with circumspection, so as to prepare beforehand for him material for his formation, and to liken his form to an archetypal beauty, and, setting before him a mark for which he is to come into being, to make for him a nature appropriate and allied to the operations, and suitable for the object in hand.

IV. THAT THE CONSTRUCTION OF MAN THROUGHOUT SIGNIFIES HIS RULING POWER

1. For as in our own life artificers fashion a tool in the way suitable to its use, so the best Artificer made our nature as it were a formation fit for the exercise of royalty, preparing it at once by superior advantages of soul, and by the very form of the body, to be such as to be adapted for royalty: for the soul immediately shows its royal and exalted character, far removed as it is from the lowliness of private station, in that it owns no lord, and is self-governed, swayed autocratically by its own will; for to whom else does this belong than to a king? And further, besides these facts, the fact that it is the image of that Nature which rules over all means nothing else than this, that our nature was created to be royal from the first. For as, in men's ordinary use, those who make images of princes both mould the figure of their form, and represent along with this the royal rank by the vesture of purple, and even the likeness is commonly spoken of as "a king," so the human nature also, as it was made to rule the rest, was, by its likeness to the King of all, made as it were a living image, partaking with the archetype both in rank and in name, not vested in purple, nor giving indication of its rank by sceptre and diadem (for the archetype itself is not arrayed with these), but instead of the purple robe, clothed in virtue, which is in truth the most royal of all raiment, and in place of the sceptre, leaning on the bliss of immortality, and instead of the royal diadem, decked with the crown of righteousness; so that it is shown to be perfectly like to the beauty of its archetype in all that belongs to the dignity of royalty.

V. THAT MAN IS A LIKENESS OF THE DIVINE SOVEREIGNTY

1. It is true, indeed, that the Divine beauty is not adorned with any shape or endowment of form, by any beauty of colour, but is contemplated as excellence in unspeakable bliss. As then painters transfer human forms to their pictures by the means of certain colours, laying on their copy the proper and corresponding tints, so that the beauty of the original may be accurately transferred to the likeness, so I would have you understand that our Maker also, painting the portrait to resemble His own beauty, by the addition of virtues, as it were with colours, shows in us His own sovereignty: and manifold and varied are the tints, so to say, by which His true form is portrayed: not red, or white , or the blending of these, whatever it may be called, nor a touch of black that paints the eyebrow and the eye, and shades, by some combination, the depressions in the figure, and all such arts which the hands of painters contrive, but instead of these, purity, freedom from passion, blessedness, alienation

from all evil, and all those attributes of the like kind which help to form in men the likeness of God: with such hues as these did the Maker of His own image mark our nature.

2. And if you were to examine the other points also by which the Divine beauty is expressed, you will find that to them too the likeness in the image which we present is perfectly preserved. The Godhead is mind and word: for "in the beginning was the Word " and the followers of Paul "have the mind of Christ" which "speaks" in them : humanity too is not far removed from these: you see in yourself word and understanding, an imitation of the very Mind and Word. Again, God is love, and the fount of love: for this the great John declares, that "love is of God," and "God is love ": the Fashioner of our nature has made this to be our feature too: for "hereby," He says, "shall all men know that ye are my disciples, if ye love one another ":—thus, if this be absent, the whole stamp of the likeness is transformed. The Deity beholds and hears all things, and searches all things out: you too have the power of apprehension of things by means of sight and hearing, and the understanding that inquires into things and searches them out.

VI. AN EXAMINATION OF THE KINDRED OF MIND TO NATURE: WHEREIN, BY WAY OF DIGRESSION, IS REFUTED THE DOCTRINE OF THE ANOMOEANS

1. And let no one suppose me to say that the Deity is in touch with existing things in a manner resembling human operation, by means of different faculties. For it is impossible to conceive in the simplicity of the Godhead the varied and diverse nature of the apprehensive operation: not even in our own case are the faculties which apprehend things numerous, although we are in touch with those things which affect our life in many ways by means of our senses; for there is one faculty, the implanted mind itself, which passes through each of the organs of sense and grasps the things beyond: this it is that, by means of the eyes, beholds what is seen; this it is that, by means of hearing, understands what is said; that is content with what is to our taste, and turns from what is unpleasant; that uses the hand for whatever it wills, taking hold or rejecting by its means, using the help of the organ for this purpose precisely as it thinks expedient.

2. If in men, then, even though the organs formed by nature for purposes of perception may be different, that which operates and moves by means of all, and uses each appropriately for the object before it, is one and the same, not changing its nature by the differences of operations, how could any one suspect multiplicity of essence in God on the ground of His varied powers? for "He

that made the eye," as the prophet says, and "that planted the ear ," stamped on human nature these operations to be as it were significant characters, with reference to their models in Himself: for He says, "Let us make man in our image ."

3. But what, I would ask, becomes of the heresy of the Anomoeans? what will they say to this utterance? how will they defend the vanity of their dogma in view of the words cited? Will they say that it is possible that one image should be made like to different forms? if the Son is in nature unlike the Father, how comes it that the likeness He forms of the different natures is one? for He Who said, "Let us make after our image," and by the plural signification revealed the Holy Trinity, would not, if the archetypes were unlike one another, have mentioned the image in the singular: for it would be impossible that there should be one likeness displayed of things which do not agree with one another: if the natures were different he would assuredly have begun their images also differently, making the appropriate image for each: but since the image is one, while the archetype is not one, who is so far beyond the range of understanding as not to know that the things which are like the same thing, surely resemble one another? Therefore He says (the word, it may be, cutting short this wickedness at the very formation of human life), "Let us make man in our image, after our likeness."

VII. WHY MAN IS DESTITUTE OF NATURAL WEAPONS AND COVERING

1. But what means the uprightness of his figure? and why is it that those powers which aid life do not naturally belong to his body? but man is brought into life bare of natural covering, an unarmed and poor being, destitute of all things useful, worthy, according to appearances, of pity rather than of admiration, not armed with prominent horns or sharp claws, nor with hoofs nor with teeth, nor possessing by nature any deadly venom in a sting,—things such as most animals have in their own power for defence against those who do them harm: his body is not protected with a covering of hair: and yet possibly it was to be expected that he who was promoted to rule over the rest of the creatures should be defended by nature with arms of his own so that he might not need assistance from others for his own security. Now, however, the lion, the boar, the tiger, the leopard, and all the like have natural power sufficient for their safety: and the bull has his horn, the hare his speed, the deer his leap and the certainty of his sight, and another beast has bulk, others a proboscis, the birds have their wings, and the bee her sting, and generally in all there is some protective power implanted by nature: but man alone of all is slower than the

beasts that are swift of foot, smaller than those that are of great bulk, more defenceless than those that are protected by natural arms; and how, one will say, has such a being obtained the sovereignty over all things?

2. Well, I think it would not be at all hard to show that what seems to be a deficiency of our nature is a means for our obtaining dominion over the subject creatures. For if man had had such power as to be able to outrun the horse in swiftness, and to have a foot that, from its solidity, could not be worn out, but was strengthened by hoofs or claws of some kind, and to carry upon him horns and stings and claws, he would be, to begin with, a wild-looking and formidable creature, if such things grew with his body: and moreover he would have neglected his rule over the other creatures if he had no need of the co-operation of his subjects; whereas now, the needful services of our life are divided among the individual animals that are under our sway, for this reason—to make our dominion over them necessary.

3. It was the slowness and difficult motion of our body that brought the horse to supply our need, and tamed him: it was the nakedness of our body that made necessary our management of sheep, which supplies the deficiency of our nature by its yearly produce of wool: it was the fact that we import from others the supplies for our living which subjected beasts of burden to such service: furthermore, it was the fact that we cannot eat grass like cattle which brought the ox to render service to our life, who makes our living easy for us by his own labour; and because we needed teeth and biting power to subdue some of the other animals by grip of teeth, the dog gave, together with his swiftness, his own jaw to supply our need, becoming like a live sword for man; and there has been discovered by men iron, stronger and more penetrating than prominent horns or sharp claws, not, as those things do with the beasts, always growing naturally with us, but entering into alliance with us for the time, and for the rest abiding by itself: and to compensate for the crocodile's scaly hide, one may make that very hide serve as armour, by putting it on his skin upon occasion: or, failing that, art fashions iron for this purpose too, which, when it has served him for a time for war, leaves the man-at-arms once more free from the burden in time of peace: and the wing of the birds, too, ministers to our life, so that by aid of contrivance we are not left behind even by the speed of wings: for some of them become tame and are of service to those who catch birds, and by their means others are by contrivance subdued to serve our needs: moreover art contrives to make our arrows feathered, and by means of the bow gives us for our needs the speed of wings: while the fact that our feet are easily hurt and worn in travelling makes necessary the aid

which is given by the subject animals: for hence it comes that we fit shoes to our feet.

VIII. WHY MAN'S FORM IS UPRIGHT; AND THAT HANDS WERE GIVEN HIM BECAUSE OF REASON; WHEREIN ALSO IS A SPECULATION ON THE DIFFERENCE OF SOULS

1. But man's form is upright, and extends aloft towards heaven, and looks upwards: and these are marks of sovereignty which show his royal dignity. For the fact that man alone among existing things is such as this, while all others bow their bodies downwards, clearly points to the difference of dignity between those which stoop beneath his sway and that power which rises above them: for all the rest have the foremost limbs of their bodies in the form of feet, because that which stoops needs something to support it: but in the formation of man these limbs were made hands, for the upright body found one base, supporting its position securely on two feet, sufficient for its needs.

2. Especially do these ministering hands adapt themselves to the requirements of the reason: indeed if one were to say that the ministration of hands is a special property of the rational nature, he would not be entirely wrong; and that not only because his thought turns to the common and obvious fact that we signify our reasoning by means of the natural employment of our hands in written characters. It is true that this fact, that we speak by writing, and, in a certain way, converse by the aid of our hands, preserving sounds by the forms of the alphabet, is not unconnected with the endowment of reason; but I am referring to something else when I say that the hands co-operate with the bidding of reason.

3. Let us, however, before discussing this point, consider the matter we passed over (for the subject of the order of created things almost escaped our notice), why the growth of things that spring from the earth takes precedence, and the irrational animals come next, and then, after the making of these, comes man: for it may be that we learn from these facts not only the obvious thought, that grass appeared to the Creator useful for the sake of the animals, while the animals were made because of man, and that for this reason, before the animals there was made their food, and before man that which was to minister to human life.

4. But it seems to me that by these facts Moses reveals a hidden doctrine, and secretly delivers that wisdom concerning the soul, of which the learning that is without had indeed some imagination, but no clear comprehension. His discourse then hereby teaches us that the power of life and soul may be considered in three divisions. For one is only a power of growth and nutrition sup-

plying what is suitable for the support of the bodies that are nourished, which is called the vegetative soul, and is to be seen in plants; for we may perceive in growing plants a certain vital power destitute of sense; and there is another form of life besides this, which, while it includes the form above mentioned, is also possessed in addition of the power of management according to sense; and this is to be found in the nature of the irrational animals: for they are not only the subjects of nourishment and growth, but also have the activity of sense and perception. But perfect bodily life is seen in the rational (I mean the human) nature, which both is nourished and endowed with sense, and also partakes of reason and is ordered by mind.

5. We might make a division of our subject in some such way as this. Of things existing, part are intellectual, part corporeal. Let us leave alone for the present the division of the intellectual according to its properties, for our argument is not concerned with these. Of the corporeal, part is entirely devoid of life, and part shares in vital energy. Of a living body, again, part has sense conjoined with life, and part is without sense: lastly, that which has sense is again divided into rational and irrational. For this reason the lawgiver says that after inanimate matter (as a sort of foundation for the form of animate things), this vegetative life was made, and had earlier existence in the growth of plants: then he proceeds to introduce the genesis of those creatures which are regulated by sense: and since, following the same order, of those things which have obtained life in the flesh, those which have sense can exist by themselves even apart from the intellectual nature, while the rational principle could not be embodied save as blended with the sensitive,—for this reason man was made last after the animals, as nature advanced in an orderly course to perfection. For this rational animal, man, is blended of every form of soul; he is nourished by the vegetative kind of soul, and to the faculty of growth was added that of sense, which stands midway, if we regard its peculiar nature, between the intellectual and the more material essence being as much coarser than the one as it is more refined than the other: then takes place a certain alliance and commixture of the intellectual essence with the subtle and enlightened element of the sensitive nature: so that man consists of these three: as we are taught the like thing by the apostle in what he says to the Ephesians , praying for them that the complete grace of their "body and soul and spirit" may be preserved at the coming of the Lord; using, the word "body" for the nutritive part, and denoting the sensitive by the word "soul," and the intellectual by "spirit." Likewise too the Lord instructs the scribe in the Gospel that he should set before every commandment that love to God which is exercised with all the heart and soul and mind : for here also it seems to me that the phrase indicates

the same difference, naming the more corporeal existence "heart," the intermediate "soul," and the higher nature, the intellectual and mental faculty, "mind."

6. Hence also the apostle recognizes three divisions of dispositions, calling one "carnal," which is busied with the belly and the pleasures connected with it, another "natural ," which holds a middle position with regard to virtue and vice, rising above the one, but without pure participation in the other; and another "spiritual," which perceives the perfection of godly life: wherefore he says to the Corinthians, reproaching their indulgence in pleasure and passion, "Ye are carnal ," and incapable of receiving the more perfect doctrine; while elsewhere, making a comparison of the middle kind with the perfect, he says, "but the natural man receiveth not the things of the Spirit: for they are foolishness unto him: but he that is spiritual judgeth all things, yet he himself is judged of no man ." As, then, the natural man is higher than the carnal, by the same measure also the spiritual man rises above the natural.

7. If, therefore, Scripture tells us that man was made last, after every animate thing, the lawgiver is doing nothing else than declaring to us the doctrine of the soul, considering that what is perfect comes last, according to a certain necessary sequence in the order of things: for in the rational are included the others also, while in the sensitive there also surely exists the vegetative form, and that again is conceived only in connection with what is material: thus we may suppose that nature makes an ascent as it were by steps—I mean the various properties of life—from the lower to the perfect form.

8 . Now since man is a rational animal, the instrument of his body must be made suitable for the use of reason ; as you may see musicians producing their music according to the form of their instruments, and not piping with harps nor harping upon flutes, so it must needs be that the organization of these instruments of ours should be adapted for reason, that when struck by the vocal organs it might be able to sound properly for the use of words. For this reason the hands were attached to the body; for though we can count up very many uses in daily life for which these skilfully contrived and helpful instruments, our hands, that easily follow every art and every operation, alike in war and peace , are serviceable, yet nature added them to our body pre-eminently for the sake of reason. For if man were destitute of hands, the various parts of his face would certainly have been arranged like those of the quadrupeds, to suit the purpose of his feeding: so that its form would have been lengthened out and pointed towards the nostrils, and his lips would have projected from his mouth, lumpy, and stiff, and thick, fitted for taking up the grass, and his tongue would either have lain between his teeth, of a kind to match his lips,

fleshy, and hard, and rough, assisting his teeth to deal with what came under his grinder, or it would have been moist and hanging out at the side like that of dogs and other carnivorous beasts, projecting through the gaps in his jagged row of teeth. If, then, our body had no hands, how could articulate sound have been implanted in it, seeing that the form of the parts of the mouth would not have had the configuration proper for the use of speech, so that man must of necessity have either bleated, or "baaed," or barked, or neighed, or bellowed like oxen or asses, or uttered some bestial sound? but now, as the hand is made part of the body, the mouth is at leisure for the service of the reason. Thus the hands are shown to be the property of the rational nature, the Creator having thus devised by their means a special advantage for reason.

IX. THAT THE FORM OF MAN WAS FRAMED TO SERVE AS AN INSTRUMENT FOR THE USE OF REASON

1. Now since our Maker has bestowed upon our formation a certain Godlike grace, by implanting in His image the likeness of His own excellences, for this reason He gave, of His bounty, His other good gifts to human nature; but mind and reason we cannot strictly say that He gave, but that He imparted them, adding to the image the proper adornment of His own nature. Now since the mind is a thing intelligible and incorporeal, its grace would have been incommunicable and isolated, if its motion were not manifested by some contrivance. For this cause there was still need of this instrumental organization, that it might, like a plectrum, touch the vocal organs and indicate by the quality of the notes struck, the motion within.

2. And as some skilled musician, who may have been deprived by some affection of his own voice, and yet wish to make his skill known, might make melody with voices of others, and publish his art by the aid of flutes or of the lyre, so also the human mind being a discoverer of all sorts of conceptions, seeing that it is unable, by the mere soul, to reveal to those who hear by bodily senses the motions of its understanding, touches, like some skilful composer, these animated instruments, and makes known its hidden thoughts by means of the sound produced upon them.

3. Now the music of the human instrument is a sort of compound of flute and lyre, sounding together in combination as in a concerted piece of music. For the breath, as it is forced up from the air-receiving vessels through the windpipe, when the speaker's impulse to utterance attunes the harmony to sound, and as it strikes against the internal protuberances which divide this flute-like passage in a circular arrangement, imitates in a way the sound uttered

through a flute, being driven round and round by the membranous projections. But the palate receives the sound from below in its own concavity, and dividing the sound by the two passages that extend to the nostrils, and by the cartilages about the perforated bone, as it were by some scaly protuberance, makes its resonance louder; while the cheek, the tongue, the mechanism of the pharynx by which the chin is relaxed when drawn in, and tightened when extended to a point—all these in many different ways answer to the motion of the plectrum upon the strings, varying very quickly, as occasion requires, the arrangement of the tones; and the opening and closing of the lips has the same effect as players produce when they check the breath of the flute with their fingers according to the measure of the tune.

X. THAT THE MIND WORKS BY MEANS OF THE SENSES

1. As the mind then produces the music of reason by means of our instrumental construction, we are born rational, while, as I think, we should not have had the gift of reason if we had had to employ our lips to supply the need of the body—the heavy and toilsome part of the task of providing food. As things are, however, our hands appropriate this ministration to themselves, and leave the mouth available for the service of reason.

2 . The operation of the instrument , however, is twofold; one for the production of sound, the other for the reception of concepts from without; and the one faculty does not blend with the other, but abides in the operation for which it was appointed by nature, not interfering with its neighbour either by the sense of hearing undertaking to speak, or by the speech undertaking to hear; for the latter is always uttering something, while the ear, as Solomon somewhere says, is not filled with continual hearing .

3. That point as to our internal faculties which seems to me to be even in a special degree matter for wonder, is this:—what is the extent of that inner receptacle into which flows everything that is poured in by our hearing? who are the recorders of the sayings that are brought in by it? what sort of storehouses are there for the concepts that are being put in by our hearing? and how is it, that when many of them, of varied kinds, are pressing one upon another, there arises no confusion and error in the relative position of the things that are laid up there? And one may have the like feeling of wonder also with regard to the operation of sight; for by it also in like manner the mind apprehends those things which are external to the body, and draws to itself the images of phenomena, marking in itself the impressions of the things which are seen.

4. And just as if there were some extensive city receiving all comers by different entrances, all will not congregate at any particular place, but some will go to the market, some to the houses, others to the churches, or the streets, or lanes, or the theatres, each according to his own inclination,—some such city of our mind I seem to discern established in us, which the different entrances through the senses keep filling, while the mind, distinguishing and examining each of the things that enters, ranks them in their proper departments of knowledge.

5. And as, to follow the illustration of the city, it may often be that those who are of the same family and kindred do not enter by the same gate, coming in by different entrances, as it may happen, but are none the less, when they come within the circuit of the wall, brought together again, being on close terms with each other (and one may find the contrary happen; for those who are strangers and mutually unknown often take one entrance to the city, yet their community of entrance does not bind them together; for even when they are within they can be separated to join their own kindred); something of the same kind I seem to discern in the spacious territory of our mind; for often the knowledge which we gather from the different organs of sense is one, as the same object is divided into several parts in relation to the senses; and again, on the contrary, we may learn from some one sense many and varied things which have no affinity one with another.

6. For instance—for it is better to make our argument clear by illustration—let us suppose that we are making some inquiry into the property of tastes—what is sweet to the sense, and what is to be avoided by tasters. We find, then, by experience, both the bitterness of gall and the pleasant character of the quality of honey; but when these facts are known, the knowledge is one which is given to us (the same thing being introduced to our understanding in several ways) by taste, smell, hearing, and often by touch and sight. For when one sees honey, and hears its name, and receives it by taste, and recognizes its odour by smell, and tests it by touch, he recognizes the same thing by means of each of his senses.

7. On the other hand we get varied and multiform information by some one sense, for as hearing receives all sorts of sounds, and our visual perception exercises its operation by beholding things of different kinds—for it lights alike on black and white, and all things that are distinguished by contrariety of colour,—so with taste, with smell, with perception by touch; each implants in us by means of its own perceptive power the knowledge of things of every kind.

XI. THAT THE NATURE OF MIND IS INVISIBLE

1. What then is, in its own nature, this mind that distributes itself into faculties of sensation, and duly receives, by means of each, the knowledge of things? That it is something else besides the senses, I suppose no reasonable man doubts; for if it were identical with sense, it would reduce the proper character of the operations carried on by sense to one, on the ground that it is itself simple, and that in what is simple no diversity is to be found. Now however, as all agree that touch is one thing and smell another, and as the rest of the senses are in like manner so situated with regard to each other as to exclude intercommunion or mixture, we must surely suppose, since the mind is duly present in each case, that it is something else besides the sensitive nature, so that no variation may attach to a thing intelligible.

2. "Who hath known the mind of the Lord ?" the apostle asks; and I ask further, who has understood his own mind? Let those tell us who consider the nature of God to be within their comprehension, whether they understand themselves—if they know the nature of their own mind. "It is manifold and much compounded." How then can that which is intelligible be composite? or what is the mode of mixture of things that differ in kind? Or, "It is simple, and incomposite." How then is it dispersed into the manifold divisions of the senses? how is there diversity in unity? how is unity maintained in diversity?

3. But I find the solution of these difficulties by recourse to the very utterance of God; for He says, "Let us make man in our image, after our likeness ." The image is properly an image so long as it fails in none of those attributes which we perceive in the archetype; but where it falls from its resemblance to the prototype it ceases in that respect to be an image; therefore, since one of the attributes we contemplate in the Divine nature is incomprehensibility of essence, it is clearly necessary that in this point the image should be able to show its imitation of the archetype.

4. For if, while the archetype transcends comprehension, the nature of the image were comprehended, the contrary character of the attributes we behold in them would prove the defect of the image; but since the nature of our mind, which is the likeness of the Creator evades our knowledge, it has an accurate resemblance to the superior nature, figuring by its own unknowableness the incomprehensible Nature.

XII. AN EXAMINATION OF THE QUESTION WHERE THE RULING PRINCIPLE IS TO BE CONSIDERED TO RESIDE; WHEREIN ALSO IS A DISCUSSION OF TEARS AND LAUGHTER, AND A PHYSIOLOGICAL SPECULATION AS TO THE INTER-RELATION OF MATTER, NATURE, AND MIND

1. Let there be an end, then, of all the vain and conjectural discussion of those who confine the intelligible energy to certain bodily organs; of whom some lay it down that the ruling principle is in the heart, while others say that the mind resides in the brain, strengthening such opinions by some plausible superficialities. For he who ascribes the principal authority to the heart makes its local position evidence of his argument (because it seems that it somehow occupies the middle position in the body), on the ground that the motion of the will is easily distributed from the centre to the whole body, and so proceeds to operation; and he makes the troublesome and passionate disposition of man a testimony for his argument, because such affections seem to move this part sympathetically. Those, on the other hand, who consecrate the brain to reasoning, say that the head has been built by nature as a kind of citadel of the whole body, and that in it the mind dwells like a king, with a bodyguard of senses surrounding it like messengers and shield-bearers. And these find a sign of their opinion in the fact that the reasoning of those who have suffered some injury to the membrane of the brain is abnormally distorted, and that those whose heads are heavy with intoxication ignore what is seemly.

2. Each of those who uphold these views puts forward some reasons of a more physical character on behalf of his opinion concerning the ruling principle. One declares that the motion which proceeds from the understanding is in some way akin to the nature of fire, because fire and the understanding are alike in perpetual motion; and since heat is allowed to have its source in the region of the heart, he says on this ground that the motion of mind is compounded with the mobility of heat, and asserts that the heart, in which heat is enclosed, is the receptacle of the intelligent nature. The other declares that the cerebral membrane (for so they call the tissue that surrounds the brain) is as it were a foundation or root of all the senses, and hereby makes good his own argument, on the ground that the intellectual energy cannot have its seat save in that part where the ear, connected with it, comes into concussion with the sounds that fall upon it, and the sight (which naturally belongs to the hollow of the place where the eyes are situated) makes its internal representation by means of the images that fall upon the pupils, while the qualities of scents are discerned in it by being drawn in through the nose, and the sense of taste is tried by the test of the cerebral membrane, which sends down from itself, by

the veterbrae of the neck, sensitive nerve-processes to the isthmoidal passage, and unites them with the muscles there.

3. I admit it to be true that the intellectual part of the soul is often disturbed by prevalence of passions; and that the reason is blunted by some bodily accident so as to hinder its natural operation; and that the heart is a sort of source of the fiery element in the body, and is moved in correspondence with the impulses of passion; and moreover, in addition to this, I do not reject (as I hear very much the same account from those who spend their time on anatomical researches) the statement that the cerebral membrane (according to the theory of those who take such a physiological view), enfolding in itself the brain, and steeped in the vapours that issue from it, forms a foundation for the senses; yet I do not hold this for a proof that the incorporeal nature is bounded by any limits of place.

4. Certainly we are aware that mental aberrations do not arise from heaviness of head alone, but skilled physicians declare that our intellect is also weakened by the membranes that underlie the sides being affected by disease, when they call the disease frenzy, since the name given to those membranes is phrenes. And the sensation resulting from sorrow is mistakenly supposed to arise at the heart; for while it is not the heart, but the entrance of the belly that is pained, people ignorantly refer the affection to the heart. Those, however, who have carefully studied the affections in question give some such account as follows:—by a compression and closing of the pores, which naturally takes place over the whole body in a condition of grief, everything that meets a hindrance in its passage is driven to the cavities in the interior of the body, and hence also (as the respiratory organs too are pressed by what surrounds them), the drawing of breath often becomes more violent under the influence of nature endeavouring to widen what has been contracted, so as to open out the compressed passages; and such breathing we consider a symptom of grief and call it a groan or a shriek. That, moreover, which appears to oppress the region of the heart is a painful affection, not of the heart, but of the entrance of the stomach, and occurs from the same cause (I mean, that of the compression of the pores), as the vessel that contains the bile, contracting, pours that bitter and pungent juice upon the entrance of the stomach; and a proof of this is that the complexion of those in grief becomes sallow and jaundiced, as the bile pours its own juice into the veins by reason of excessive pressure.

5. Furthermore, the opposite affection, that, I mean, of mirth and laughter, contributes to establish the argument; for the pores of the body, in the case of those who are dissolved in mirth by hearing something pleasant, are also somehow dissolved and relaxed. Just as in the former case the slight and insen-

sible exhalations of the pores are checked by grief, and, as they compress the internal arrangement of the higher viscera, drive up towards the head and the cerebral membrane the humid vapour which, being retained in excess by the cavities of the brain, is driven out by the pores at its base , while the closing of the eyelids expels the moisture in the form of drops (and the drop is called a tear), so I would have you think that when the pores, as a result of the contrary condition, are unusually widened, some air is drawn in through them into the interior, and thence again expelled by nature through the passage of the mouth, while all the viscera (and especially, as they say, the liver) join in expelling this air by a certain agitation and throbbing motion; whence it comes that nature, contriving to give facility for the exit of the air, widens the passage of the mouth, extending the cheeks on either side round about the breath; and the result is called laughter.

6. We must not, then, on this account ascribe the ruling principle any more to the liver than we must think, because of the heated state of the blood about the heart in wrathful dispositions, that the seat of the mind is in the heart; but we must refer these matters to the character of our bodily organization, and consider that the mind is equally in contact with each of the parts according to a kind of combination which is indescribable.

7. Even if any should allege to us on this point the Scripture which claims the ruling principle for the heart, we shall not receive the statement without examination; for he who makes mention of the heart speaks also of the reins, when he says, "God trieth the hearts and reins" ; so that they must either confine the intellectual principle to the two combined or to neither.

8. And although I am aware that the intellectual energies are blunted, or even made altogether ineffective in a certain condition of the body, I do not hold this a sufficient evidence for limiting the faculty of the mind by any particular place, so that it should be forced out of its proper amount of free space by any inflammations that may arise in the neighbouring parts of the body (for such an opinion is a corporeal one, that when the receptacle is already occupied by something placed in it, nothing else can find place there); for the intelligible nature neither dwells in the empty spaces of bodies, nor is extruded by encroachments of the flesh; but since the whole body is made like some musical instrument, just as it often happens in the case of those who know how to play, but are unable, because the unfitness of the instrument does not admit of their art, to show their skill (for that which is destroyed by time, or broken by a fall, or rendered useless by rust or decay, is mute and inefficient, even if it be breathed upon by one who may be an excellent artist in flute-playing); so too the mind, passing over the whole instrument, and touch-

ing each of the parts in a mode corresponding to its intellectual activities, according to its nature, produces its proper effect on those parts which are in a natural condition, but remains inoperative and ineffective upon those which are unable to admit the movement of its art; for the mind is somehow naturally adapted to be in close relation with that which is in a natural condition, but to be alien from that which is removed from nature.

9. And here, I think there is a view of the matter more close to nature, by which we may learn something of the more refined doctrines. For since the most beautiful and supreme good of all is the Divinity Itself, to which incline all things that have a tendency towards what is beautiful and good , we therefore say that the mind, as being in the image of the most beautiful, itself also remains in beauty and goodness so long as it partakes as far as is possible in its likeness to the archetype; but if it were at all to depart from this it is deprived of that beauty in which it was. And as we said that the mind was adorned by the likeness of the archetypal beauty, being formed as though it were a mirror to receive the figure of that which it expresses, we consider that the nature which is governed by it is attached to the mind in the same relation, and that it too is adorned by the beauty that the mind gives, being, so to say, a mirror of the mirror; and that by it is swayed and sustained the material element of that existence in which the nature is contemplated.

10. Thus so long as one keeps in touch with the other, the communication of the true beauty extends proportionally through the whole series, beautifying by the superior nature that which comes next to it; but when there is any interruption of this beneficent connection, or when, on the contrary, the superior comes to follow the inferior, then is displayed the misshapen character of matter, when it is isolated from nature (for in itself matter is a thing without form or structure), and by its shapelessness is also destroyed that beauty of nature with which it is adorned through the mind; and so the transmission of the ugliness of matter reaches through the nature to the mind itself, so that the image of God is no longer seen in the figure expressed by that which was moulded according to it; for the mind, setting the idea of good like a mirror behind the back, turns off the incident rays of the effulgence of the good, and it receives into itself the impress of the shapelessness of matter.

11. And in this way is brought about the genesis of evil, arising through the withdrawal of that which is beautiful and good. Now all is beautiful and good that is closely related to the First Good; but that which departs from its relation and likeness to this is certainly devoid of beauty and goodness. If, then, according to the statement we have been considering, that which is truly good is one, and the mind itself also has its power of being beautiful and good, in so

far as it is in the image of the good and beautiful, and the nature, which is sustained by the mind, has the like power, in so far as it is an image of the image, it is hereby shown that our material part holds together, and is upheld when it is controlled by nature; and on the other hand is dissolved and disorganized when it is separated from that which upholds and sustains it, and is dissevered from its conjunction with beauty and goodness.

12. Now such a condition as this does not arise except when there takes place an overturning of nature to the opposite state, in which the desire has no inclination for beauty and goodness, but for that which is in need of the adorning element; for it must needs be that that which is made like to matter, destitute as matter is of form of its own, should be assimilated to it in respect of the absence alike of form and of beauty.

13. We have, however, discussed these points in passing, as following on our argument, since they were introduced by our speculation on the point before us; for the subject of enquiry was, whether the intellectual faculty has its seat in any of the parts of us, or extends equally over them all; for as for those who shut up the mind locally in parts of the body, and who advance for the establishment of this opinion of theirs the fact that the reason has not free course in the case of those whose cerebral membranes are in an unnatural condition, our argument showed that in respect of every part of the compound nature of man, whereby every man has some natural operation, the power of the soul remains equally ineffective if the part does not continue in its natural condition. And thus there came into our argument, following out this line of thought, the view we have just stated, by which we learn that in the compound nature of man the mind is governed by God, and that by it is governed our material life, provided the latter remains in its natural state, but if it is perverted from nature it is alienated also from that operation which is carried on by the mind.

14. Let us return however once more to the point from which we started—that in those who are not perverted from their natural condition by some affection, the mind exercises its own power, and is established firmly in those who are in sound health, but on the contrary is powerless in those who do not admit its operation; for we may confirm our opinion on these matters by yet other arguments: and if it is not tedious for those to hear who are already wearied with our discourse, we shall discuss these matters also, so far as we are able, in a few words.

XIII. A RATIONALE OF SLEEP, OF YAWNING, AND OF DREAMS

1. This life of our bodies, material and subject to flux, always advancing by way of motion, finds the power of its being in this, that it never rests from its motion: and as some river, flowing on by its own impulse, keeps the channel in which it runs well filled, yet is not seen in the same water always at the same place, but part of it glides away while part comes flowing on, so, too, the material element of our life here suffers change in the continuity of its succession of opposites by way of motion and flux, so that it never can desist from change, but in its inability to rest keeps up unceasingly its motion alternating by like ways : and if it should ever cease moving it will assuredly have cessation also of its being.

2. For instance, emptying succeeds fulness, and on the other hand after emptiness comes in turn a process of filling: sleep relaxes the strain of waking, and, again, awakening braces up what had become slack: and neither of these abides continually, but both give way, each at the other's coming; nature thus by their interchange so renewing herself as, while partaking of each in turn, to pass from the one to the other without break. For that the living creature should always be exerting itself in its operations produces a certain rupture and severance of the overstrained part; and continual quiescence of the body brings about a certain dissolution and laxity in its frame: but to be in touch with each of these at the proper times in a moderate degree is a staying-power of nature, which, by continual transference to the opposed states, gives herself in each of them rest from the other. Thus she finds the body on the strain through wakefulness, and devises relaxation for the strain by means of sleep, giving the perceptive faculties rest for the time from their operations, loosing them like horses from the chariots after the race.

3. Further, rest at proper times is necessary for the framework of the body, that the nutriment may be diffused over the whole body through the passages which it contains, without any strain to hinder its progress. For just as certain misty vapours are drawn up from the recesses of the earth when it is soaked with rain, whenever the sun heats it with rays of any considerable warmth, so a similar result happens in the earth that is in us, when the nutriment within is heated up by natural warmth; and the vapours, being naturally of upward tendency and airy nature, and aspiring to that which is above them, come to be in the region of the head like smoke penetrating the joints of a wall: then they are dispersed thence by exhalation to the passages of the organs of sense, and by them the senses are of course rendered inactive, giving way to the transit of these vapours. For the eyes are pressed upon by the eyelids when some leaden instrument , as it were (I mean such a weight as that I have spoken of), lets

down the eyelid upon the eyes; and the hearing, being dulled by these same vapours, as though a door were placed upon the acoustic organs, rests from its natural operation: and such a condition is sleep, when the sense is at rest in the body, and altogether ceases from the operation of its natural motion, so that the digestive processes of nutriment may have free course for transmission by the vapours through each of the passages.

4. And for this reason, if the apparatus of the organs of sense should be closed and sleep hindered by some occupation, the nervous system, becoming filled with the vapours, is naturally and spontaneously extended so that the part which has had its density increased by the vapours is rarefied by the process of extension, just as those do who squeeze the water out of clothes by vehement wringing: and, seeing that the parts about the pharynx are somewhat circular, and nervous tissue abounds there, whenever there is need for the expulsion from that part of the density of the vapours—since it is impossible that the part which is circular in shape should be separated directly, but only by being distended in the outline of its circumference—for this reason, by checking the breath in a yawn the chin is moved downwards so as to leave a hollow to the uvula, and all the interior parts being arranged in the figure of a circle, that smoky denseness which had been detained in the neighbouring parts is emitted together with the exit of the breath. And often the like may happen even after sleep when any portion of those vapours remains in the region spoken of undigested and unexhaled.

5. Hence the mind of man clearly proves its claim to connection with his nature, itself also co-operating and moving with the nature in its sound and waking state, but remaining unmoved when it is abandoned to sleep, unless any one supposes that the imagery of dreams is a motion of the mind exercised in sleep. We for our part say that it is only the conscious and sound action of the intellect which we ought to refer to mind; and as to the fantastic nonsense which occurs to us in sleep, we suppose that some appearances of the operations of the mind are accidentally moulded in the less rational part of the soul; for the soul, being by sleep dissociated from the senses, is also of necessity outside the range of the operations of the mind; for it is through the senses that the union of mind with man takes place; therefore when the senses are at rest, the intellect also must needs be inactive; and an evidence of this is the fact that the dreamer often seems to be in absurd and impossible situations, which would not happen if the soul were then guided by reason and intellect.

6. It seems to me, however, that when the soul is at rest so far as concerns its more excellent faculties (so far, I mean, as concerns the operations of mind and sense), the nutritive part of it alone is operative during sleep, and that

some shadows and echoes of those things which happen in our waking moments—of the operations both of sense and of intellect—which are impressed upon it by that part of the soul which is capable of memory, that these, I say, are pictured as chance will have it, some echo of memory still lingering in this division of the soul.

7. With these, then, the man is beguiled, not led to acquaintance with the things that present themselves by any train of thought, but wandering among confused and inconsequent delusions. But just as in his bodily operations, while each of the parts individually acts in some way according to the power which naturally resides in it, there arises also in the limb that is at rest a state sympathetic with that which is in motion, similarly in the case of the soul, even if one part is at rest and another in motion, the whole is affected in sympathy with the part; for it is not possible that the natural unity should be in any way severed, though one of the faculties included in it is in turn supreme in virtue of its active operation. But as, when men are awake and busy, the mind is supreme, and sense ministers to it, yet the faculty which regulates the body is not dissociated from them (for the mind furnishes the food for its wants, the sense receives what is furnished, and the nutritive faculty of the body appropriates to itself that which is given to it), so in sleep the supremacy of these faculties is in some way reversed in us, and while the less rational becomes supreme, the operation of the other ceases indeed, yet is not absolutely extinguished; but while the nutritive faculty is then busied with digestion during sleep, and keeps all our nature occupied with itself, the faculty of sense is neither entirely severed from it (for that cannot be separated which has once been naturally joined), nor yet can its activity revive, as it is hindered by the inaction during sleep of the organs of sense; and by the same reasoning (the mind also being united to the sensitive part of the soul) it would follow that we should say that the mind moves with the latter when it is in motion, and rests with it when it is quiescent.

8. As naturally happens with fire when it is heaped over with chaff, and no breath fans the flame—it neither consumes what lies beside it, nor is entirely quenched, but instead of flame it rises to the air through the chaff in the form of smoke; yet if it should obtain any breath of air, it turns the smoke to flame—in the same way the mind when hidden by the inaction of the senses in sleep is neither able to shine out through them, nor yet is quite extinguished, but has, so to say, a smouldering activity, operating to a certain extent, but unable to operate farther.

9. Again, as a musician, when he touches with the plectrum the slackened strings of a lyre, brings out no orderly melody (for that which is not stretched

will not sound), but his hand frequently moves skilfully, bringing the plectrum to the position of the notes so far as place is concerned, yet there is no sound, except that he produces by the vibration of the strings a sort of uncertain and indistinct hum; so in sleep the mechanism of the senses being relaxed, the artist is either quite inactive, if the instrument is completely relaxed by satiety or heaviness; or will act slackly and faintly, if the instrument of the senses does not fully admit of the exercise of its art.

10. For this cause memory is confused, and foreknowledge, though rendered doubtful by uncertain veils, is imaged in shadows of our waking pursuits, and often indicates to us something of what is going to happen: for by its subtlety of nature the mind has some advantage, in ability to behold things, over mere corporeal grossness; yet it cannot make its meaning clear by direct methods, so that the information of the matter in hand should be plain and evident, but its declaration of the future is ambiguous and doubtful,—what those who interpret such things call an "enigma."

11. So the butler presses the cluster for Pharaoh's cup: so the baker seemed to carry his baskets; each supposing himself in sleep to be engaged in those services with which he was busied when awake: for the images of their customary occupations imprinted on the prescient element of their soul, gave them for a time the power of foretelling, by this sort of prophecy on the part of the mind, what should come to pass.

12. But if Daniel and Joseph and others like them were instructed by Divine power, without any confusion of perception, in the knowledge of things to come, this is nothing to the present statement; for no one would ascribe this to the power of dreams, since he will be constrained as a consequence to suppose that those Divine appearances also which took place in wakefulness were not a miraculous vision but a result of nature brought about spontaneously. As then, while all men are guided by their own minds, there are some few who are deemed worthy of evident Divine communication; so, while the imagination of sleep naturally occurs in a like and equivalent manner for all, some, not all, share by means of their dreams in some more Divine manifestation: but to all the rest even if a foreknowledge of anything does occur as a result of dreams, it occurs in the way we have spoken of.

13. And again, if the Egyptian and the Assyrian king were guided by God to the knowledge of the future, the dispensation wrought by their means is a different thing: for it was necessary that the hidden wisdom of the holy men should be made known, that each of them might not pass his life without profit to the state. For how could Daniel have been known for what he was, if the soothsayers and magicians had not been unequal to the task of discovering

the dream? And how could Egypt have been preserved while Joseph was shut up in prison, if his interpretation of the dream had not brought him to notice? Thus we must reckon these cases as exceptional, and not class them with common dreams.

14. But this ordinary seeing of dreams is common to all men, and arises in our fancies in different modes and forms: for either there remain, as we have said, in the reminiscent part of the soul, the echoes of daily occupations; or, as often happens, the constitution of dreams is framed with regard to such and such a condition of the body: for thus the thirsty man seems to be among springs, the man who is in need of food to be at a feast, and the young man in the heat of youthful vigour is beset by fancies corresponding to his passion.

15. I also knew another cause of the fancies of sleep, when attending one of my relations attacked by frenzy; who being annoyed by food being given him in too great quantity for his strength, kept crying out and finding fault with those who were about him for filling intestines with dung and putting them upon him: and when his body was rapidly tending to perspire he blamed those who were with him for having water ready to wet him with as he lay: and he did not cease calling out till the result showed the meaning of these complaints: for all at once a copious sweat broke out over his body, and a relaxation of the bowels explained the weight in the intestines. The same condition then which, while his sober judgment was dulled by disease, his nature underwent, being sympathetically affected by the condition of the body—not being without perception of what was amiss, but being unable clearly to express its pain, by reason of the distraction resulting from the disease—this, probably, if the intelligent principle of the soul were lulled to rest, not from infirmity but by natural sleep, might appear as a dream to one similarly situated, the breaking out of perspiration being expressed by water, and the pain occasioned by the food, by the weight of intestines.

16. This view also is taken by those skilled in medicine, that according to the differences of complaints the visions of dreams appear differently to the patients: that the visions of those of weak stomach are of one kind, those of persons suffering from injury to the cerebral membrane of another, those of persons in fevers of yet another; that those of patients suffering from bilious and from phlegmatic affections are diverse, and those again of plethoric patients, and of patients in wasting disease, are different; whence we may see that the nutritive and vegetative faculty of the soul has in it by commixture some seed of the intelligent element, which is in some sense brought into likeness to the particular state of the body, being adapted in its fancies according to the complaint which has seized upon it.

17. Moreover, most men's dreams are conformed to the state of their character: the brave man's fancies are of one kind, the coward's of another; the wanton man's dreams of one kind, the continent man's of another; the liberal man and the avaricious man are subject to different fancies; while these fancies are nowhere framed by the intellect, but by the less rational disposition of the soul, which forms even in dreams the semblances of those things to which each is accustomed by the practice of his waking hours.

XIV. THAT THE MIND IS NOT IN A PART OF THE BODY; WHEREIN ALSO IS A DISTINCTION OF THE MOVEMENTS OF THE BODY AND OF THE SOUL

1. But we have wandered far from our subject, for the purpose of our argument was to show that the mind is not restricted to any part of the body, but is equally in touch with the whole, producing its motion according to the nature of the part which is under its influence. There are cases, however, in which the mind even follows the bodily impulses, and becomes, as it were, their servant; for often the bodily nature takes the lead by introducing either the sense of that which gives pain or the desire for that which gives pleasure, so that it may be said to furnish the first beginnings, by producing in us the desire for food, or, generally, the impulse towards some pleasant thing; while the mind, receiving such an impulse, furnishes the body by its own intelligence with the proper means towards the desired object. Such a condition, indeed, does not occur in all, save in those of a somewhat slavish disposition, who bring the reason into bondage to the impulses of their nature and pay servile homage to the pleasures of sense by allowing them the alliance of their mind; but in the case of more perfect men this does not happen; for the mind takes the lead, and chooses the expedient course by reason and not by passion, while their nature follows in the tracks of its leader.

2. But since our argument discovered in our vital faculty three different varieties—one which receives nourishment without perception, another which at once receives nourishment and is capable of perception, but is without the reasoning activity, and a third rational, perfect, and co-extensive with the whole faculty—so that among these varieties the advantage belongs to the intellectual,—let no one suppose on this account that in the compound nature of man there are three souls welded together, contemplated each in its own limits, so that one should think man's nature to be a sort of conglomeration of several souls. The true and perfect soul is naturally one, the intellectual and immaterial, which mingles with our material nature by the agency of the senses; but all that is of material nature, being subject to mutation and altera-

tion, will, if it should partake of the animating power, move by way of growth: if, on the contrary, it should fall away from the vital energy, it will reduce its motion to destruction.

3. Thus, neither is there perception without material substance, nor does the act of perception take place without the intellectual faculty.

XV. THAT THE SOUL PROPER, IN FACT AND NAME, IS THE RATIONAL SOUL, WHILE THE OTHERS ARE CALLED SO EQUIVOCALLY; WHEREIN ALSO IS THIS STATEMENT, THAT THE POWER OF THE MIND EXTENDS THROUGHOUT THE WHOLE BODY IN FITTING CONTACT WITH EVERY PART

1. Now, if some things in creation possess the nutritive faculty, and others again are regulated by the perceptive faculty, while the former have no share of perception nor the latter of the intellectual nature, and if for this reason any one is inclined to the opinion of a plurality of souls, such a man will be positing a variety of souls in a way not in accordance with their distinguishing definition. For everything which we conceive among existing things, if it be perfectly that which it is, is also properly called by the name it bears: but of that which is not every respect what it is called, the appellation also is vain. For instance:—if one were to show us true bread, we say that he properly applies the name to the subject: but if one were to show us instead that which had been made of stone to resemble the natural bread, which had the same shape, and equal size, and similarity of colour, so as in most points to be the same with its prototype, but which yet lacks the power of being food, on this account we say that the stone receives the name of "bread," not properly, but by a misnomer, and all things which fall under the same description, which are not absolutely what they are called, have their name from a misuse of terms.

2. Thus, as the soul finds its perfection in that which is intellectual and rational, everything that is not so may indeed share the name of "soul," but is not really soul, but a certain vital energy associated with the appellation of "soul ." And for this reason also He Who gave laws on every matter, gave the animal nature likewise, as not far removed from this vegetative life , for the use of man, to be for those who partake of it instead of herbs:—for He says, "Ye shall eat all kinds of flesh even as the green herb ;" for the perceptive energy seems to have but a slight advantage over that which is nourished and grows without it. Let this teach carnal men not to bind their intellect closely to the phenomena of sense, but rather to busy themselves with their spiritual advantages, as the true soul is found in these, while sense has equal power also among the brute creation.

3. The course of our argument, however, has diverged to another point: for the subject of our speculation was not the fact that the energy of mind is of more dignity among the attributes we conceive in man than the material element of his being, but the fact that the mind is not confined to any one part of us, but is equally in all and through all, neither surrounding anything without, nor being enclosed within anything: for these phrases are properly applied to casks or other bodies that are placed one inside the other; but the union of the mental with the bodily presents a connection unspeakable and inconceivable,—not being within it (for the incorporeal is not enclosed in a body), nor yet surrounding it without (for that which is incorporeal does not include anything), but the mind approaching our nature in some inexplicable and incomprehensible way, and coming into contact with it, is to be regarded as both in it and around it, neither implanted in it nor enfolded with it, but in a way which we cannot speak or think, except so far as this, that while the nature prospers according to its own order, the mind is also operative; but if any misfortune befalls the former, the movement of the intellect halts correspondingly.

XVI. A CONTEMPLATION OF THE DIVINE UTTERANCE WHICH SAID—"LET US MAKE MAN AFTER OUR IMAGE AND LIKENESS"; WHEREIN IS EXAMINED WHAT IS THE DEFINITION OF THE IMAGE, AND HOW THE PASSIBLE AND MORTAL IS LIKE TO THE BLESSED AND IMPASSIBLE, AND HOW IN THE IMAGE THERE ARE MALE AND FEMALE, SEEING THESE ARE NOT IN THE PROTOTYPE

1. Let us now resume our consideration of the Divine word, "Let us make man in our image, after our likeness ." How mean and how unworthy of the majesty of man are the fancies of some heathen writers, who magnify humanity, as they supposed, by their comparison of it to this world! for they say that man is a little world, composed of the same elements with the universe. Those who bestow on human nature such praise as this by a high-sounding name, forget that they are dignifying man with the attributes of the gnat and the mouse: for they too are composed of these four elements,—because assuredly about the animated nature of every existing thing we behold a part, greater or less, of those elements without which it is not natural that any sensitive being should exist. What great thing is there, then, in man's being accounted a representation and likeness of the world,—of the heaven that passes away, of the earth that changes, of all things that they contain, which pass away with the departure of that which compasses them round?

2. In what then does the greatness of man consist, according to the doctrine of the Church? Not in his likeness to the created world, but in his being in the image of the nature of the Creator.

3. What therefore, you will perhaps say, is the definition of the image? How is the incorporeal likened to body? how is the temporal like the eternal? that which is mutable by change like to the immutable? that which is subject to passion and corruption to the impassible and incorruptible? that which constantly dwells with evil, and grows up with it, to that which is absolutely free from evil? there is a great difference between that which is conceived in the archetype, and a thing which has been made in its image: for the image is properly so called if it keeps its resemblance to the prototype; but if the imitation be perverted from its subject, the thing is something else, and no longer an image of the subject.

4. How then is man, this mortal, passible, shortlived being, the image of that nature which is immortal, pure, and everlasting? The true answer to this question, indeed, perhaps only the very Truth knows: but this is what we, tracing out the truth so far as we are capable by conjectures and inferences, apprehend concerning the matter. Neither does the word of God lie when it says that man was made in the image of God, nor is the pitiable suffering of man's nature like to the blessedness of the impassible Life: for if any one were to compare our nature with God, one of two things must needs be allowed in order that the definition of the likeness may be apprehended in both cases in the same terms,—either that the Deity is passible, or that humanity is impassible: but if neither the Deity is passible nor our nature free from passion, what other account remains whereby we may say that the word of God speaks truly, which says that man was made in the image of God?

5. We must, then, take up once more the Holy Scripture itself, if we may perhaps find some guidance in the question by means of what is written. After saying, "Let us make man in our image," and for what purposes it was said "Let us make him," it adds this saying:—"and God created man; in the image of God created He him; male and female created He them ." We have already said in what precedes, that this saying was uttered for the destruction of heretical impiety, in order that being instructed that the Only-begotten God made man in the image of God, we should in no wise distinguish the Godhead of the Father and the Son, since Holy Scripture gives to each equally the name of God,—to Him Who made man, and to Him in Whose image he was made.

6. However, let us pass by our argument upon this point: let us turn our inquiry to the question before us,—how it is that while the Deity is in bliss,

and humanity is in misery, the latter is yet in Scripture called "like" the former?

7. We must, then, examine the words carefully: for we find, if we do so, that that which was made "in the image" is one thing, and that which is now manifested in wretchedness is another. "God created man," it says; "in the image of God created He him ." There is an end of the creation of that which was made "in the image": then it makes a resumption of the account of creation, and says, "male and female created He them." I presume that every one knows that this is a departure from the Prototype: for "in Christ Jesus," as the apostle says, "there is neither male nor female ." Yet the phrase declares that man is thus divided.

8. Thus the creation of our nature is in a sense twofold: one made like to God, one divided according to this distinction: for something like this the passage darkly conveys by its arrangement, where it first says, "God created man, in the image of God created He him ," and then, adding to what has been said, "male and female created He them ,"—a thing which is alien from our conceptions of God.

9. I think that by these words Holy Scripture conveys to us a great and lofty doctrine; and the doctrine is this. While two natures—the Divine and incorporeal nature, and the irrational life of brutes—are separated from each other as extremes, human nature is the mean between them: for in the compound nature of man we may behold a part of each of the natures I have mentioned,—of the Divine, the rational and intelligent element, which does not admit the distinction of male and female; of the irrational, our bodily form and structure, divided into male and female: for each of these elements is certainly to be found in all that partakes of human life. That the intellectual element, however, precedes the other, we learn as from one who gives in order an account of the making of man; and we learn also that his community and kindred with the irrational is for man a provision for reproduction. For he says first that "God created man in the image of God" (showing by these words, as the Apostle says, that in such a being there is no male or female): then he adds the peculiar attributes of human nature, "male and female created He them ."

10. What, then, do we learn from this? Let no one, I pray, be indignant if I bring from far an argument to bear upon the present subject. God is in His own nature all that which our mind can conceive of good;—rather, transcending all good that we can conceive or comprehend. He creates man for no other reason than that He is good; and being such, and having this as His reason for entering upon the creation of our nature, He would not exhibit the power of His goodness in an imperfect form, giving our nature some one of the things at

His disposal, and grudging it a share in another: but the perfect form of goodness is here to be seen by His both bringing man into being from nothing, and fully supplying him with all good gifts: but since the list of individual good gifts is a long one, it is out of the question to apprehend it numerically. The language of Scripture therefore expresses it concisely by a comprehensive phrase, in saying that man was made "in the image of God": for this is the same as to say that He made human nature participant in all good; for if the Deity is the fulness of good, and this is His image, then the image finds its resemblance to the Archetype in being filled with all good.

11. Thus there is in us the principle of all excellence, all virtue and wisdom, and every higher thing that we conceive: but pre-eminent among all is the fact that we are free from necessity, and not in bondage to any natural power, but have decision in our own power as we please; for virtue is a voluntary thing, subject to no dominion: that which is the result of compulsion and force cannot be virtue.

12. Now as the image bears in all points the semblance of the archetypal excellence, if it had not a difference in some respect, being absolutely without divergence it would no longer be a likeness, but will in that case manifestly be absolutely identical with the Prototype. What difference then do we discern between the Divine and that which has been made like to the Divine? We find it in the fact that the former is uncreate, while the latter has its being from creation: and this distinction of property brings with it a train of other properties; for it is very certainly acknowledged that the uncreated nature is also immutable, and always remains the same, while the created nature cannot exist without change; for its very passage from nonexistence to existence is a certain motion and change of the non-existent transmuted by the Divine purpose into being.

13. As the Gospel calls the stamp upon the coin "the image of Caesar ," whereby we learn that in that which was fashioned to resemble Caesar there was resemblance as to outward look, but difference as to material, so also in the present saying, when we consider the attributes contemplated both in the Divine and human nature, in which the likeness consists, to be in the place of the features, we find in what underlies them the difference which we behold in the uncreated and in the created nature.

14. Now as the former always remains the same, while that which came into being by creation had the beginning of its existence from change, and has a kindred connection with the like mutation, for this reason He Who, as the prophetical writing says, "knoweth all things before they be ," following out, or rather perceiving beforehand by His power of foreknowledge what, in a state of

independence and freedom, is the tendency of the motion of man's will,—as He saw, I say, what would be, He devised for His image the distinction of male and female, which has no reference to the Divine Archetype, but, as we have said, is an approximation to the less rational nature.

15. The cause, indeed, of this device, only those can know who were eye-witnesses of the truth and ministers of the Word; but we, imagining the truth, as far as we can, by means of conjectures and similitudes, do not set forth that which occurs to our mind authoritatively, but will place it in the form of a theoretical speculation before our kindly hearers.

16. What is it then which we understand concerning these matters? In saying that "God created man" the text indicates, by the indefinite character of the term, all mankind; for was not Adam here named together with the creation, as the history tells us in what follows ? yet the name given to the man created is not the particular, but the general name: thus we are led by the employment of the general name of our nature to some such view as this—that in the Divine foreknowledge and power all humanity is included in the first creation; for it is fitting for God not to regard any of the things made by Him as indeterminate, but that each existing thing should have some limit and measure prescribed by the wisdom of its Maker.

17. Now just as any particular man is limited by his bodily dimensions, and the peculiar size which is conjoined with the superficies of his body is the measure of his separate existence, so I think that the entire plenitude of humanity was included by the God of all, by His power of foreknowledge, as it were in one body, and that this is what the text teaches us which says, "God created man, in the image of God created He him." For the image is not in part of our nature, nor is the grace in any one of the things found in that nature, but this power extends equally to all the race: and a sign of this is that mind is implanted alike in all: for all have the power of understanding and deliberating, and of all else whereby the Divine nature finds its image in that which was made according to it: the man that was manifested at the first creation of the world, and he that shall be after the consummation of all, are alike: they equally bear in themselves the Divine image .

18. For this reason the whole race was spoken of as one man, namely, that to God's power nothing is either past or future, but even that which we expect is comprehended, equally with what is at present existing, by the all-sustaining energy. Our whole nature, then, extending from the first to the last, is, so to say, one image of Him Who is; but the distinction of kind in male and female was added to His work last, as I suppose, for the reason which follows .

XVII. WHAT WE MUST ANSWER TO THOSE WHO RAISE THE QUESTION—"IF PROCREATION IS AFTER SIN, HOW WOULD SOULS HAVE COME INTO BEING IF THE FIRST OF MANKIND HAD REMAINED SINLESS ?"

1. It is better for us however, perhaps, rather to inquire, before investigating this point, the solution of the question put forward by our adversaries; for they say that before the sin there is no account of birth, or of travail, or of the desire that tends to procreation, but when they were banished from Paradise after their sin, and the woman was condemned by the sentence of travail, Adam thus entered with his consort upon the intercourse of married life, and then took place the beginning of procreation. If, then, marriage did not exist in Paradise, nor travail, nor birth, they say that it follows as a necessary conclusion that human souls would not have existed in plurality had not the grace of immortality fallen away to mortality, and marriage preserved our race by means of descendants, introducing the offspring of the departing to take their place, so that in a certain way the sin that entered into the world was profitable for the life of man: for the human race would have remained in the pair of the first-formed, had not the fear of death impelled their nature to provide succession.

2. Now here again the true answer, whatever it may be, can be clear to those only who, like Paul, have been instructed in the mysteries of Paradise; but our answer is as follows. When the Sadducees once argued against the doctrine of the resurrection, and brought forward, to establish their own opinion, that woman of many marriages, who had been wife to seven brethren, and thereupon inquired whose wife she will be after the resurrection, our Lord answered their argument so as not only to instruct the Sadducees, but also to reveal to all that come after them the mystery of the resurrection-life: "for in the resurrection," He says, "they neither marry, nor are given in marriage; neither can they die any more, for they are equal to the angels, and are the children of God, being the children of the resurrection ." Now the resurrection promises us nothing else than the restoration of the fallen to their ancient state; for the grace we look for is a certain return to the first life, bringing back again to Paradise him who was cast out from it. If then the life of those restored is closely related to that of the angels, it is clear that the life before the transgression was a kind of angelic life, and hence also our return to the ancient condition of our life is compared to the angels. Yet while, as has been said, there is no marriage among them, the armies of the angels are in countless myriads; for so Daniel declared in his visions: so, in the same way, if there had not come upon us as the result of sin a change for the worse, and removal from equality with the angels, neither should we have needed marriage that we might multi-

ply; but whatever the mode of increase in the angelic nature is (unspeakable and inconceivable by human conjectures, except that it assuredly exists), it would have operated also in the case of men, who were "made a little lower than the angels ," to increase mankind to the measure determined by its Maker.

3. But if any one finds a difficulty in an inquiry as to the manner of the generation of souls, had man not needed the assistance of marriage, we shall ask him in turn, what is the mode of the angelic existence, how they exist in countless myriads, being one essence, and at the same time numerically many; for we shall be giving a fit answer to one who raises the question how man would have been without marriage, if we say, "as the angels are without marriage;" for the fact that man was in a like condition with them before the transgression is shown by the restoration to that state.

4. Now that we have thus cleared up these matters, let us return to our former point,—how it was that after the making of His image God contrived for His work the distinction of male and female. I say that the preliminary speculation we have completed is of service for determining this question; for He Who brought all things into being and fashioned Man as a whole by His own will to the Divine image, did not wait to see the number of souls made up to its proper fulness by the gradual additions of those coming after; but while looking upon the nature of man in its entirety and fulness by the exercise of His foreknowledge, and bestowing upon it a lot exalted and equal to the angels, since He saw beforehand by His all-seeing power the failure of their will to keep a direct course to what is good, and its consequent declension from the angelic life, in order that the multitude of human souls might not be cut short by its fall from that mode by which the angels were increased and multiplied,—for this reason, I say, He formed for our nature that contrivance for increase which befits those who had fallen into sin, implanting in mankind, instead of the angelic majesty of nature, that animal and irrational mode by which they now succeed one another.

5. Hence also, it seems to me, the great David pitying the misery of man mourns over his nature with such words as these, that, "man being in honour knew it not" (meaning by "honour" the equality with the angels), therefore, he says, "he is compared to the beasts that have no understanding, and made like unto them ." For he truly was made like the beasts, who received in his nature the present mode of transient generation, on account of his inclination to material things.

XVIII. THAT OUR IRRATIONAL PASSIONS HAVE THEIR RISE FROM KINDRED WITH IRRATIONAL NATURE

1. For I think that from this beginning all our passions issue as from a spring, and pour their flood over man's life; and an evidence of my words is the kinship of passions which appears alike in ourselves and in the brutes; for it is not allowable to ascribe the first beginnings of our constitutional liability to passion to that human nature which was fashioned in the Divine likeness; but as brute life first entered into the world, and man, for the reason already mentioned, took something of their nature (I mean the mode of generation), he accordingly took at the same time a share of the other attributes contemplated in that nature; for the likeness of man to God is not found in anger, nor is pleasure a mark of the superior nature; cowardice also, and boldness, and the desire of gain, and the dislike of loss, and all the like, are far removed from that stamp which indicates Divinity.

2. These attributes, then, human nature took to itself from the side of the brutes; for those qualities with which brute life was armed for self-preservation, when transferred to human life, became passions; for the carnivorous animals are preserved by their anger, and those which breed largely by their love of pleasure; cowardice preserves the weak, fear that which is easily taken by more powerful animals, and greediness those of great bulk; and to miss anything that tends to pleasure is for the brutes a matter of pain. All these and the like affections entered man's composition by reason of the animal mode of generation.

3. I may be allowed to describe the human image by comparison with some wonderful piece of modelling. For, as one may see in models those carved shapes which the artificers of such things contrive for the wonder of beholders, tracing out upon a single head two forms of faces; so man seems to me to bear a double likeness to opposite things—being moulded in the Divine element of his mind to the Divine beauty, but bearing, in the passionate impulses that arise in him, a likeness to the brute nature; while often even his reason is rendered brutish, and obscures the better element by the worse through its inclination and disposition towards what is irrational; for whenever a man drags down his mental energy to these affections, and forces his reason to become the servant of his passions, there takes place a sort of conversion of the good stamp in him into the irrational image, his whole nature being traced anew after that design, as his reason, so to say, cultivates the beginnings of his passions, and gradually multiplies them; for once it lends its co-operation to passion, it produces a plenteous and abundant crop of evils.

4. Thus our love of pleasure took its beginning from our being made like to the irrational creation, and was increased by the transgressions of men, becom-

ing the parent of so many varieties of sins arising from pleasure as we cannot find among the irrational animals. Thus the rising of anger in us is indeed akin to the impulse of the brutes; but it grows by the alliance of thought: for thence come malignity, envy, deceit, conspiracy, hypocrisy; all these are the result of the evil husbandry of the mind; for if the passion were divested of the aid it receives from thought, the anger that is left behind is short-lived and not sustained, like a bubble, perishing straightway as soon as it comes into being. Thus the greediness of swine introduces covetousness, and the high spirit of the horse becomes the origin of pride; and all the particular forms that proceed from the want of reason in brute nature become vice by the evil use of the mind.

5. So, likewise, on the contrary, if reason instead assumes sway over such emotions, each of them is transmuted to a form of virtue; for anger produces courage, terror caution, fear obedience, hatred aversion from vice, the power of love the desire for what is truly beautiful; high spirit in our character raises our thought above the passions, and keeps it from bondage to what is base; yea, the great Apostle, even, praises such a form of mental elevation when he bids us constantly to "think those things that are above ;" and so we find that every such motion, when elevated by loftiness of mind, is conformed to the beauty of the Divine image.

6. But the other impulse is greater, as the tendency of sin is heavy and downward; for the ruling element of our soul is more inclined to be dragged downwards by the weight of the irrational nature than is the heavy and earthy element to be exalted by the loftiness of the intellect; hence the misery that encompasses us often causes the Divine gift to be forgotten, and spreads the passions of the flesh, like some ugly mask, over the beauty of the image.

7. Those, therefore, are in some sense excusable, who do not admit, when they look upon such cases, that the Divine form is there; yet we may behold the Divine image in men by the medium of those who have ordered their lives aright. For if the man who is subject to passion, and carnal, makes it incredible that man was adorned, as it were, with Divine beauty, surely the man of lofty virtue and pure from pollution will confirm you in the better conception of human nature.

8. For instance (for it is better to make our argument clear by an illustration), one of those noted for wickedness—some Jechoniah, say, or some other of evil memory—has obliterated the beauty of his nature by the pollution of wickedness; yet in Moses and in men like him the form of the image was kept pure. Now where the beauty of the form has not been obscured, there is made plain the faithfulness of the saying that man is an image of God.

9. It may be, however, that some one feels shame at the fact that our life, like that of the brutes, is sustained by food, and for this reason deems man unworthy of being supposed to have been framed in the image of God; but he may expect that freedom from this function will one day be bestowed upon our nature in the life we look for; for, as the Apostle says, "the Kingdom of God is not meat and drink ;" and the Lord declared that "man shall not live by bread alone, but by every word that proceedeth out of the mouth of God ." Further, as the resurrection holds forth to us a life equal with the angels, and with the angels there is no food, there is sufficient ground for believing that man, who will live in like fashion with the angels, will be released from such a function.

XIX. TO THOSE WHO SAY THAT THE ENJOYMENT OF THE GOOD THINGS WE LOOK FOR WILL AGAIN CONSIST IN MEAT AND DRINK, BECAUSE IT IS WRITTEN THAT BY THESE MEANS MAN AT FIRST LIVED IN PARADISE

1. But some one perhaps will say that man will not be returning to the same form of life, if as it seems, we formerly existed by eating, and shall hereafter be free from that function. I, however, when I hear the Holy Scripture, do not understand only bodily meat, or the pleasure of the flesh; but I recognize another kind of food also, having a certain analogy to that of the body, the enjoyment of which extends to the soul alone: "Eat of my bread ," is the bidding of Wisdom to the hungry; and the Lord declares those blessed who hunger for such food as this, and says, "If any man thirst, let him come unto Me, and drink": and "drink ye joy ," is the great Isaiah's charge to those who are able to hear his sublimity. There is a prophetic threatening also against those worthy of vengeance, that they shall be punished with famine; but the "famine" is not a lack of bread and water, but a failure of the word:—"not a famine of bread, nor a thirst for water, but a famine of hearing the word of the Lord ."

2. We ought, then, to conceive that the fruit in Eden was something worthy of God's planting (and Eden is interpreted to mean "delight"), and not to doubt that man was hereby nourished: nor should we at all conceive, concerning the mode of life in Paradise, this transitory and perishable nutriment: "of every tree of the garden," He says, "thou mayest freely eat ."

3. Who will give to him that has a healthful hunger that tree that is in Paradise, which includes all good, which is named "every tree," in which this passage bestows on man the right to share? for in the universal and transcendent saying every form of good is in harmony with itself, and the whole is one. And who will keep me back from that tasting of the tree which is of mixed and

doubtful kind? for surely it is clear to all who are at all keen-sighted what that "every" tree is whose fruit is life, and what again that mixed tree is whose end is death: for He Who presents ungrudgingly the enjoyment of "every" tree, surely by some reason and forethought keeps man from participation in those which are of doubtful kind.

4. It seems to me that I may take the great David and the wise Solomon as my instructors in the interpretation of this text: for both understand the grace of the permitted delight to be one,—that very actual Good, which in truth is "every" good;—David, when he says, "Delight thou in the Lord ," and Solomon, when he names Wisdom herself (which is the Lord) "a tree of life ."

5. Thus the "every" tree of which the passage gives food to him who was made in the likeness of God, is the same with the tree of life; and there is opposed to this tree another tree, the food given by which is the knowledge of good and evil:—not that it bears in turn as fruit each of these things of opposite significance, but that it produces a fruit blended and mixed with opposite qualities, the eating of which the Prince of Life forbids, and the serpent counsels, that he may prepare an entrance for death: and he obtained credence for his counsel, covering over the fruit with a fair appearance and the show of pleasure, that it might be pleasant to the eyes and stimulate the desire to taste.

XX. WHAT WAS THE LIFE IN PARADISE, AND WHAT WAS THE FORBIDDEN TREE ?

1. What then is that which includes the knowledge of good and evil blended together, and is decked with the pleasures of sense? I think I am not aiming wide of the mark in employing, as a starting-point for my speculation, the sense of "knowable ." It is not, I think, "science" which the Scripture here means by "knowledge"; but I find a certain distinction, according to Scriptural use, between "knowledge" and "discernment": for to "discern" skilfully the good from the evil, the Apostle says is a mark of a more perfect condition and of "exercised senses ," for which reason also he bids us "prove all things ," and says that "discernment" belongs to the spiritual man : but "knowledge" is not always to be understood of skill and acquaintance with anything, but of the disposition towards what is agreeable,—as "the Lord knoweth them that are His "; and He says to Moses, "I knew thee above all "; while of those condemned in their wickedness He Who knows all things says, "I never knew you ."

2. The tree, then, from which comes this fruit of mixed knowledge, is among those things which are forbidden; and that fruit is combined of oppo-

site qualities, which has the serpent to commend it, it may be for this reason, that the evil is not exposed in its nakedness, itself appearing in its own proper nature—for wickedness would surely fail of its effect were it not decked with some fair colour to entice to the desire of it him whom it deceives—but now the nature of evil is in a manner mixed, keeping destruction like some snare concealed in its depths, and displaying some phantom of good in the deceitfulness of its exterior. The beauty of the substance seems good to those who love money: yet "the love of money is a root of all evil ": and who would plunge into the unsavoury mud of wantonness, were it not that he whom this bait hurries into passion thinks pleasure a thing fair and acceptable? so, too, the other sins keep their destruction hidden, and seem at first sight acceptable, and some deceit makes them earnestly sought after by unwary men instead of what is good.

3. Now since the majority of men judge the good to lie in that which gratifies the senses, and there is a certain identity of name between that which is, and that which appears to be "good,"—for this reason that desire which arises towards what is evil, as though towards good, is called by Scripture "the knowledge of good and evil;" "knowledge," as we have said, expressing a certain mixed disposition. It speaks of the fruit of the forbidden tree not as a thing absolutely evil (because it is decked with good), nor as a thing purely good (because evil is latent in it), but as compounded of both, and declares that the tasting of it brings to death those who touch it; almost proclaiming aloud the doctrine that the very actual good is in its nature simple and uniform, alien from all duplicity or conjunction with its opposite, while evil is many-coloured and fairly adorned, being esteemed to be one thing and revealed by experience as another, the knowledge of which (that is, its reception by experience) is the beginning and antecedent of death and destruction.

4. It was because he saw this that the serpent points out the evil fruit of sin, not showing the evil manifestly in its own nature (for man would not have been deceived by manifest evil), but giving to what the woman beheld the glamour of a certain beauty, and conjuring into its taste the spell of a sensual pleasure, he appeared to her to speak convincingly: "and the woman saw," it says, "that the tree was good for food, and that it was pleasant to the eyes to behold, and fair to see; and she took of the fruit thereof and did eat ," and that eating became the mother of death to men. This, then, is that fruit-bearing of mixed character, where the passage clearly expresses the sense in which the tree was called "capable of the knowledge of good and evil," because, like the evil nature of poisons that are prepared with honey, it appears to be good in so far as it affects the senses with sweetness: but in so far as it destroys him who

touches it, it is the worst of all evil. Thus when the evil poison worked its effect against man's life, then man, that noble thing and name, the image of God's nature, was made, as the prophet says, "like unto vanity ."

5. The image, therefore, properly belongs to the better part of our attributes; but all in our life that is painful and miserable is far removed from the likeness to the Divine.

XXI. THAT THE RESURRECTION IS LOOKED FOR AS A CONSEQUENCE, NOT SO MUCH FROM THE DECLARATION OF SCRIPTURE AS FROM THE VERY NECESSITY OF THINGS

1. Wickedness, however, is not so strong as to prevail over the power of good; nor is the folly of our nature more powerful and more abiding than the wisdom of God: for it is impossible that that which is always mutable and variable should be more firm and more abiding than that which always remains the same and is firmly fixed in goodness: but it is absolutely certain that the Divine counsel possesses immutability, while the changeableness of our nature does not remain settled even in evil.

2. Now that which is always in motion, if its progress be to good, will never cease moving onwards to what lies before it, by reason of the infinity of the course to be traversed:—for it will not find any limit of its object such that when it has apprehended it, it will at last cease its motion: but if its bias be in the opposite direction, when it has finished the course of wickedness and reached the extreme limit of evil, then that which is ever moving, finding no halting point for its impulse natural to itself when it has run through the lengths that can be run in wickedness, of necessity turns its motion towards good: for as evil does not extend to infinity, but is comprehended by necessary limits, it would appear that good once more follows in succession upon the limit of evil; and thus, as we have said, the ever-moving character of our nature comes to run its course at the last once more back towards good, being taught the lesson of prudence by the memory of its former misfortunes, to the end that it may never again be in like case.

3. Our course, then, will once more lie in what is good, by reason of the fact that the nature of evil is bounded by necessary limits. For just as those skilled in astronomy tell us that the whole universe is full of light, and that darkness is made to cast its shadow by the interposition of the body formed by the earth; and that this darkness is shut off from the rays of the sun, in the shape of a cone, according to the figure of the sphere-shaped body, and behind it; while the sun, exceeding the earth by a size many times as great as its own, enfolding it round about on all sides with its rays, unites at the limit of the

cone the concurrent streams of light; so that if (to suppose the case) any one had the power of passing beyond the measure to which the shadow extends, he would certainly find himself in light unbroken by darkness;—even so I think that we ought to understand about ourselves, that on passing the limit of wickedness we shall again have our conversation in light, as the nature of good, when compared with the measure of wickedness, is incalculably superabundant.

4. Paradise therefore will be restored, that tree will be restored which is in truth the tree of life;—there will be restored the grace of the image, and the dignity of rule. It does not seem to me that our hope is one for those things which are now subjected by God to man for the necessary uses of life, but one for another kingdom, of a description that belongs to unspeakable mysteries.

XXII. TO THOSE WHO SAY, "IF THE RESURRECTION IS A THING EXCELLENT AND GOOD, HOW IS IT THAT IT HAS NOT HAPPENED ALREADY, BUT IS HOPED FOR IN SOME PERIODS OF TIME?"

1. Let us give our attention, however, to the next point of our discussion. It may be that some one, giving his thought wings to soar towards the sweetness of our hope, deems it a burden and a loss that we are not more speedily placed in that good state which is above man's sense and knowledge, and is dissatisfied with the extension of the time that intervenes between him and the object of his desire. Let him cease to vex himself like a child that is discontented at the brief delay of something that gives him pleasure; for since all things are governed by reason and wisdom, we must by no means suppose that anything that happens is done without reason itself and the wisdom that is therein.

2. You will say then, What is this reason, in accordance with which the change of our painful life to that which we desire does not take place at once, but this heavy and corporeal existence of ours waits, extended to some determinate time, for the term of the consummation of all things, that then man's life may be set free as it were from the reins, and revert once more, released and free, to the life of blessedness and impassibility?

3. Well, whether our answer is near the truth of the matter, the Truth Itself may clearly know; but at all events what occurs to our intelligence is as follows. I take up then once more in my argument our first text:—God says, "Let us make man in our image, after our likeness, and God created man, in the image of God created He him ." Accordingly, the Image of God, which we behold in universal humanity, had its consummation then ; but Adam as yet was not; for the thing formed from the earth is called Adam, by etymological nomenclature, as those tell us who are acquainted with the Hebrew tongue—wherefore

also the apostle, who was specially learned in his native tongue, the tongue of the Israelites, calls the man "of the earth " choikos, as though translating the name Adam into the Greek word.

4. Man, then, was made in the image of God; that is, the universal nature, the thing like God; not part of the whole, but all the fulness of the nature together was so made by omnipotent wisdom. He saw, Who holds all limits in His grasp, as the Scripture tells us which says, "in His hand are all the corners of the earth ," He saw, "Who knoweth all things" even "before they be ," comprehending them in His knowledge, how great in number humanity will be in the sum of its individuals. But as He perceived in our created nature the bias towards evil, and the fact that after its voluntary fall from equality with the angels it would acquire a fellowship with the lower nature, He mingled, for this reason, with His own image, an element of the irrational (for the distinction of male and female does not exist in the Divine and blessed nature);—transferring, I say, to man the special attribute of the irrational formation, He bestowed increase upon our race not according to the lofty character of our creation; for it was not when He made that which was in His own image that He bestowed on man the power of increasing and multiplying; but when He divided it by sexual distinctions, then He said, "Increase and multiply, and replenish the earth ." For this belongs not to the Divine, but to the irrational element, as the history indicates when it narrates that these words were first spoken by God in the case of the irrational creatures; since we may be sure that, if He had bestowed on man, before imprinting on our nature the distinction of male and female, the power for increase conveyed by this utterance, we should not have needed this form of generation by which the brutes are generated.

5. Now seeing that the full number of men pre-conceived by the operation of foreknowledge will come into life by means of this animal generation, God, Who governs all things in a certain order and sequence,—since the inclination of our nature to what was beneath it (which He Who beholds the future equally with the present saw before it existed) made some such form of generation absolutely necessary for mankind,—therefore also foreknew the time coextensive with the creation of men, so that the extent of time should be adapted for the entrances of the pre-determined souls, and that the flux and motion of time should halt at the moment when humanity is no longer produced by means of it; and that when the generation of men is completed, time should cease together with its completion, and then should take place the restitution of all things, and with the World-Reformation humanity also

should be changed from the corruptible and earthly to the impassible and eternal.

6. And this it seems to me the Divine apostle considered when he declared in his epistle to the Corinthians the sudden stoppage of time, and the change of the things that are now moving on back to the opposite end where he says, "Behold, I show you a mystery; we shall not all sleep, but we shall all be changed, in a moment, in the twinkling of an eye, at the last trump ." For when, as I suppose, the full complement of human nature has reached the limit of the pre-determined measure, because there is no longer anything to be made up in the way of increase to the number of souls, he teaches us that the change in existing things will take place in an instant of time, giving to that limit of time which has no parts or extension the names of "a moment," and "the twinkling of an eye"; so that it will no more be possible for one who reaches the verge of time (which is the last and extreme point, from the fact that nothing is lacking to the attainment of its extremity) to obtain by death this change which takes place at a fixed period, but only when the trumpet of the resurrection sounds, which awakens the dead, and transforms those who are left in life, after the likeness of those who have undergone the resurrection change, at once to incorruptibility; so that the weight of the flesh is no longer heavy, nor does its burden hold them down to earth, but they rise aloft through the air—for, "we shall be caught up," he tells us, "in the clouds to meet the Lord in the air; and so shall we ever be with the Lord ."

7. Let him therefore wait for that time which is necessarily made co-extensive with the development of humanity. For even Abraham and the patriarchs, while they had the desire to see the promised good things, and ceased not to seek the heavenly country, as the apostle says, are yet even now in the condition of hoping for that grace, "God having provided some better thing for us," according to the words of Paul, "that they without us should not be made perfect ." If they, then, bear the delay who by faith only and by hope saw the good things "afar off" and "embraced them ," as the apostle bears witness, placing their certainty of the enjoyment of the things for which they hoped in the fact that they "judged Him faithful Who has promised ," what ought most of us to do, who have not, it may be, a hold upon the better hope from the character of our lives? Even the prophet's soul fainted with desire, and in his psalm he confesses this passionate love, saying that his "soul hath a desire and longing to be in the courts of the Lord ," even if he must needs be rejected to a place amongst the lowest, as it is a greater and more desirable thing to be last there than to be first among the ungodly tents of this life; nevertheless he was patient of the delay, deeming, indeed, the life there blessed,

and accounting a brief participation in it more desirable than "thousands" of time—for he says, "one day in Thy courts is better than thousands "—yet he did not repine at the necessary dispensation concerning existing things, and thought it sufficient bliss for man to have those good things even by way of hope; wherefore he says at the end of the Psalm, "O Lord of hosts, blessed is the man that hopeth in Thee ."

8. Neither, then, should we be troubled at the brief delay of what we hope for, but give diligence that we may not be cast out from the object of our hopes; for just as though, if one were to tell some inexperienced person beforehand, "the gathering of the crops will take place in the season of summer, and the stores will be filled, and the table abundantly supplied with food at the time of plenty," it would be a foolish man who should seek to hurry on the coming of the fruit-time, when he ought to be sowing seeds and preparing the crops for himself by diligent care; for the fruit-time will surely come, whether he wishes or not, at the appointed time; and it will be looked on differently by him who has secured for himself beforehand abundance of crops, and by him who is found by the fruit-time destitute of all preparation. Even so I think it is one's duty, as the proclamation is clearly made to all that the time of change will come, not to trouble himself about times (for He said that "it is not for us to know the times and the seasons "), nor to pursue calculations by which he will be sure to sap the hope of the resurrection in the soul; but to make his confidence in the things expected as a prop to lean on, and to purchase for himself, by good conversation, the grace that is to come.

XXIII. THAT HE WHO CONFESSES THE BEGINNING OF THE WORLD'S EXISTENCE MUST NECESSARILY ALSO AGREE AS TO ITS END

But if some one, beholding the present course of the world, by which intervals of time are marked, going on in a certain order, should say that it is not possible that the predicted stoppage of these moving things should take place, such a man clearly also does not believe that in the beginning the heaven and the earth were made by God; for he who admits a beginning of motion surely does not doubt as to its also having an end; and he who does not allow its end, does not admit its beginning either; but as it is by believing that "we understand that the worlds were framed by the word of God," as the apostle says, "so that things which are seen were not made of things which do appear ," we must use the same faith as to the word of God when He foretells the necessary stoppage of existing things.

2. The question of the "how" must, however, be put beyond the reach of our meddling; for even in the case mentioned it was "by faith" that we admitted that the thing seen was framed from things not yet apparent, omitting the search into things beyond our reach. And yet our reason suggests difficulties on many points, offering no small occasions for doubt as to the things which we believe.

3. For in that case too, argumentative men might by plausible reasoning upset our faith, so that we should not think that statement true which Holy Scripture delivers concerning the material creation, when it asserts that all existing things have their beginning of being from God. For those who abide by the contrary view maintain that matter is co-eternal with God, and employ in support of their own doctrine some such arguments as these. If God is in His nature simple and immaterial, without quantity , or size, or combination, and removed from the idea of circumscription by way of figure, while all matter is apprehended in extension measured by intervals, and does not escape the apprehension of our senses, but becomes known to us in colour, and figure, and bulk, and size, and resistance, and the other attributes belonging to it, none of which it is possible to conceive in the Divine nature,—what method is there for the production of matter from the immaterial, or of the nature that has dimensions from that which is unextended? for if these things are believed to have their existence from that source, they clearly come into existence after being in Him in some mysterious way; but if material existence was in Him, how can He be immaterial while including matter in Himself? and similarly with all the other marks by which the material nature is differentiated; if quantity exists in God, how is God without quantity? if the compound nature exists in Him, how is He simple, without parts and without combination? so that the argument forces us to think either that He is material, because matter has its existence from Him as a source; or, if one avoids this, it is necessary to suppose that matter was imported by Him ab extra for the making of the universe.

4. If, then, it was external to God, something else surely existed besides God, conceived, in respect of eternity, together with Him Who exists ungenerately; so that the argument supposes two eternal and unbegotten existences, having their being concurrently with each other—that of Him Who operates as an artificer, and that of the thing which admits this skilled operation; and if any one under pressure of this argument should assume a material substratum for the Creator of all things, what a support will the Manichaean find for his special doctrine, who opposes by virtue of ungenerateness a material existence to a Good Being. Yet we do believe that all things are of God, as we hear the

Scripture say so; and as to the question how they were in God, a question beyond our reason, we do not seek to pry into it, believing that all things are within the capacity of God's power—both to give existence to what is not, and to implant qualities at His pleasure in what is.

5. Consequently, as we suppose the power of the Divine will to be a sufficient cause to the things that are, for their coming into existence out of nothing, so too we shall not repose our belief on anything beyond probability in referring the World-Reformation to the same power. Moreover, it might perhaps be possible, by some skill in the use of words, to persuade those who raise frivolous objections on the subject of matter not to think that they can make an unanswerable attack on our statement.

XXIV. AN ARGUMENT AGAINST THOSE WHO SAY THAT MATTER IS CO-ETERNAL WITH GOD

1. For after all that opinion on the subject of matter does not turn out to be beyond what appears consistent, which declares that it has its existence from Him Who is intelligible and immaterial. For we shall find all matter to be composed of certain qualities, of which if it is divested it can, in itself, be by no means grasped by idea. Moreover in idea each kind of quality is separated from the substratum; but idea is an intellectual and not a corporeal method of examination. If, for instance, some animal or tree is presented to our notice, or any other of the things that have material existence, we perceive in our mental discussion of it many things concerning the substratum, the idea of each of which is clearly distinguished from the object we contemplate: for the idea of colour is one, of weight another; so again that of quantity and of such and such a peculiar quality of touch: for "softness," and "two cubits long," and the rest of the attributes we spoke of, are not connected in idea either with one another or with the body: each of them has conceived concerning it its own explanatory definition according to its being, having nothing in common with any other of the qualities that are contemplated in the substratum.

2. If, then, colour is a thing intelligible, and resistance also is intelligible, and so with quantity and the rest of the like properties, while if each of these should be withdrawn from the substratum, the whole idea of the body is dissolved; it would seem to follow that we may suppose the concurrence of those things, the absence of which we found to be a cause of the dissolution of the body, to produce the material nature: for as that is not a body which has not colour, and figure, and resistance, and extension, and weight, and the other properties, while each of these in its proper existence is found to be not

the body but something else besides the body, so, conversely, whenever the specified attributes concur they produce bodily existence. Yet if the perception of these properties is a matter of intellect, and the Divinity is also intellectual in nature, there is no incongruity in supposing that these intellectual occasions for the genesis of bodies have their existence from the incorporeal nature, the intellectual nature on the one hand giving being to the intellectual potentialities, and the mutual concurrence of these bringing to its genesis the material nature.

3. Let this discussion, however, be by way of digression: we must direct our discourse once more to the faith by which we accept the statement that the universe took being from nothing, and do not doubt, when we are taught by Scripture, that it will again be transformed into some other state.

XXV. HOW ONE EVEN OF THOSE WHO ARE WITHOUT MAY BE BROUGHT TO BELIEVE THE SCRIPTURE WHEN TEACHING OF THE RESURRECTION

1. Some one, perhaps, having regard to the dissolution of bodies, and judging the Deity by the measure of his own power, asserts that the idea of the resurrection is impossible, saying that it cannot be that both those things which are now in motion should become stationary, and those things which are now without motion should rise again.

2. Let such an one, however, take as the first and greatest evidence of the truth touching the resurrection the credibility of the herald who proclaims it. Now the faith of what is said derives its certainty from the result of the other predictions: for as the Divine Scripture delivers statements many and various, it is possible by examining how the rest of the utterances stand in the matter of falsehood and truth to survey also, in the light of them, the doctrine concerning the resurrection. For if in the other matters the statements are found to be false and to have failed of true fulfilment, neither is this out of the region of falsehood; but if all the others have experience to vouch for their truth, it would seem logical to esteem as true, on their account, the prediction concerning the resurrection also. Let us therefore recall one or two of the predictions that have been made, and compare the result with what was foretold, so that we may know by means of them whether the idea has a truthful aspect.

3. Who knows not how the people of Israel flourished of old, raised up against all the powers of the world; what were the palaces in the city of Jerusalem, what the walls, the towers, the majestic structure of the Temple? things that seemed worthy of admiration even to the disciples of the Lord, so that they asked the Lord to take notice of them, in their disposition to marvel, as

the Gospel history shows us, saying, "What works, and what buildings !" But He indicates to those who wondered at its present state the future desolation of the place and the disappearance of that beauty, saying that after a little while nothing of what they saw should be left. And, again, at the time of His Passion, the women followed, bewailing the unjust sentence against Him,—for they could not yet see into the dispensation of what was being done:—but He bids them be silent as to what is befalling Him, for it does not demand their tears, but to reserve their wailing and lamentation for the true time for tears, when the city should be compassed by besiegers, and their sufferings reach so great a strait that they should deem him happy who had not been born: and herein He foretold also the horrid deed of her who devoured her child, when He said that in those days the womb should be accounted blest that never bare . Where then are those palaces? where is the Temple? where are the walls? where are the defences of the towers? where is the power of the Israelites? were not they scattered in different quarters over almost the whole world? and in their overthrow the palaces also were brought to ruin.

4. Now it seems to me that the Lord foretold these things and others like them not for the sake of the matters themselves—for what great advantage to the hearers, at any rate, was the prediction of what was about to happen? they would have known by experience, even if they had not previously learnt what would come;—but in order that by these means faith on their part might follow concerning more important matters: for the testimony of facts in the former cases is also a proof of truth in the latter.

5. For just as though, if a husbandman were explaining the virtue of seeds, it were to happen that some person inexperienced in husbandry should disbelieve him, it would be sufficient as proof of his statement for the agriculturist to show him the virtue existing in one seed of those in the bushel and make it a pledge of the rest—for he who should see the single grain of wheat or barley, or whatever might chance to be the contents of the bushel, grow into an ear after being cast into the ground, would by the means of the one cease also to disbelieve concerning the others—so the truthfulness which confessedly belongs to the other statements seems to me to be sufficient also for evidence of the mystery of the resurrection.

6. Still more, however, is this the case with the experience of actual resurrection which we have learnt not so much by words as by actual facts: for as the marvel of resurrection was great and passing belief, He begins gradually by inferior instances of His miraculous power, and accustoms our faith, as it were, for the reception of the greater.

7. For as a mother who nurses her babe with due care for a time supplies milk by her breast to its mouth while still tender and soft; and when it begins to grow and to have teeth she gives it bread, not hard or such as it cannot chew, so that the tender and unpractised gums may not be chafed by rough food; but softening it with her own teeth, she makes it suitable and convenient for the powers of the eater; and then as its power increases by growth she gradually leads on the babe, accustomed to tender food, to more solid nourishment; so the Lord, nourishing and fostering with miracles the weakness of the human mind, like some babe not fully grown, makes first of all a prelude of the power of the resurrection in the case of a desperate disease, which prelude, though it was great in its achievement, yet was not such a thing that the statement of it would be disbelieved: for by "rebuking the fever" which was fiercely consuming Simon's wife's mother, He produced so great a removal of the evil as to enable her who was already expected to be near death, to "minister " to those present.

8. Next He makes a slight addition to the power, and when the nobleman's son lies in acknowledged danger of death (for so the history tells us, that he was about to die, as his father cried, "come down, ere my child die "), He again brings about the resurrection of one who was believed about to die; accomplishing the miracle with a greater act of power in that He did not even approach the place, but sent life from afar off by the force of His command.

9. Once more in what follows He ascends to higher wonders. For having set out on His way to the ruler of the synagogue's daughter, he voluntarily made a halt in His way, while making public the secret cure of the woman with an issue of blood, that in this time death might overcome the sick. When, then, the soul had just been parted from the body, and those who were wailing over the sorrow were making a tumult with their mournful cries, He raises the damsel to life again, as if from sleep, by His word of command, leading on human weakness, by a sort of path and sequence, to greater things.

10. Still in addition to these acts He exceeds them in wonder, and by a more exalted act of power prepares for men the way of faith in the resurrection. The Scripture tells us of a city called Nain in Judaea: a widow there had an only child, no longer a child in the sense of being among boys, but already passing from childhood to man's estate: the narrative calls him "a young man." The story conveys much in few words: the very recital is a real lamentation: the dead man's mother, it says, "was a widow." See you the weight of her misfortune, how the text briefly sets out the tragedy of her suffering? for what does the phrase mean? that she had no more hope of bearing sons, to cure the loss she had just sustained in him who had departed; for the woman was a widow:

she had not in her power to look to another instead of to him who was gone; for he was her only child; and how great a grief is here expressed any one may easily see who is not an utter stranger to natural feeling. Him alone she had known in travail, him alone she had nursed at her breast; he alone made her table cheerful, he alone was the cause of brightness in her home, in play, in work, in learning, in gaiety, at processions, at sports, at gatherings of youth; he alone was all that is sweet and precious in a mother's eyes. Now at the age of marriage, he was the stock of her race, the shoot of its succession, the staff of her old age. Moreover, even the additional detail of his time of life is another lament: for he who speaks of him as "a young man" tells of the flower of his faded beauty, speaks of him as just covering his face with down, not yet with a full thick beard, but still bright with the beauty of his cheeks. What then, think you, were his mother's sorrows for him? how would her heart be consumed as it were with a flame; how bitterly would she prolong her lament over him, embracing the corpse as it lay before her, lengthening out her mourning for him as far as possible, so as not to hasten the funeral of the dead, but to have her fill of sorrow! Nor does the narrative pass this by: for Jesus "when He saw her," it says, "had compassion"; "and He came and touched the bier; and they that bare him stood still;" and He said to the dead, "Young man, I say unto thee, arise ," "and He delivered him to his mother" alive. Observe that no short time had intervened since the dead man had entered upon that state, he was all but laid in the tomb; the miracle wrought by the Lord is greater, though the command is the same.

11. His miraculous power proceeds to a still more exalted act, that its display may more closely approach that miracle of the resurrection which men doubt. One of the Lord's companions and friends is ill (Lazarus is the sick man's name); and the Lord deprecates any visiting of His friend, though far away from the sick man, that in the absence of the Life, death might find room and power to do his own work by the agency of disease. The Lord informs His disciples in Galilee of what has befallen Lazarus, and also of his own setting out to him to raise him up when laid low. They, however, were exceedingly afraid on account of the fury of the Jews, thinking it a difficult and dangerous matter to turn again towards Judaea, in the midst of those who sought to slay Him: and thus, lingering and delaying, they return slowly from Galilee: but they do return, for His command prevailed, and the disciples were led by the Lord to be initiated at Bethany in the preliminary mysteries of the general resurrection. Four days had already passed since the event; all due rites had been performed for the departed; the body was hidden in the tomb: it was probably already swollen and beginning to dissolve into corruption, as the body mouldered in

the dank earth and necessarily decayed: the thing was one to turn from, as the dissolved body under the constraint of nature changed to offensiveness . At this point the doubted fact of the general resurrection is brought to proof by a more manifest miracle; for one is not raised from severe sickness, nor brought back to life when at the last breath—nor is a child just dead brought to life, nor a young man about to be conveyed to the tomb released from his bier; but a man past the prime of life, a corpse, decaying, swollen, yea already in a state of dissolution, so that even his own kinsfolk could not suffer that the Lord should draw near the tomb by reason of the offensiveness of the decayed body there enclosed, brought into life by a single call, confirms the proclamation of the resurrection, that is to say, that expectation of it as universal, which we learn by a particular experience to entertain. For as in the regeneration of the universe the Apostle tells us that "the Lord Himself will descend with a shout, with the voice of the archangel ," and by a trumpet sound raise up the dead to incorruption—so now too he who is in the tomb, at the voice of command, shakes off death as if it were a sleep, and ridding himself from the corruption that had come upon his condition of a corpse, leaps forth from the tomb whole and sound, not even hindered in his egress by the bonds of the grave-cloths round his feet and hands.

12. Are these things too small to produce faith in the resurrection of the dead? or dost thou seek that thy judgment on this point should be confirmed by yet other proofs? In truth the Lord seems to me not to have spoken in vain to them of Capernaum, when He said to Himself, as in the person of men, "Ye will surely say unto me this proverb, Physician, heal thyself .'" For it behoved Him, when He had accustomed men to the miracle of the resurrection in other bodies, to confirm His word in His own humanity. Thou sawest the thing proclaimed working in others—those who were about to die, the child which had just ceased to live, the young man at the edge of the grave, the putrefying corpse, all alike restored by one command to life. Dost thou seek for those who have come to death by wounds and bloodshed? does any feebleness of life-giving power hinder the grace in them? Behold Him Whose hands were pierced with nails: behold Him Whose side was transfixed with a spear; pass thy fingers through the print of the nails; thrust thy hand into the spear-wound ; thou canst surely guess how far within it is likely the point would reach, if thou reckonest the passage inwards by the breadth of the external scar; for the wound that gives admission to a man's hand, shows to what depth within the iron entered. If He then has been raised, well may we utter the Apostle's exclamation, "How say some that there is no resurrection of the dead ?"

13. Since, then, every prediction of the Lord is shown to be true by the testimony of events, while we not only have learnt this by His words, but also received the proof of the promise in deed, from those very persons who returned to life by resurrection, what occasion is left to those who disbelieve? Shall we not bid farewell to those who pervert our simple faith by "philosophy and vain deceit ," and hold fast to our confession in its purity, learning briefly through the prophet the mode of the grace, by his words, "Thou shalt take away their breath and they shall fail, and turn to their dust. Thou shalt send forth Thy Spirit and they shall be created, and Thou shalt renew the face of the earth ;" at which time also he says that the Lord rejoices in His works, sinners having perished from the earth: for how shall any one be called by the name of sin, when sin itself exists no longer?

XXVI. THAT THE RESURRECTION IS NOT BEYOND PROBABILITY

1. There are, however, some who, owing to the feebleness of human reasoning, judging the Divine power by the compass of our own, maintain that what is beyond our capacity is not possible even to God. They point to the disappearance of the dead of old time, and to the remains of those who have been reduced to ashes by fire; and further, besides these, they bring forward in idea the carnivorous beasts, and the fish that receives in its own body the flesh of the shipwrecked sailor, while this again in turn becomes food for men, and passes by digestion into the bulk of him who eats it: and they rehearse many such trivialities, unworthy of God's great power and authority, for the overthrow of the doctrine, arguing as though God were not able to restore to man his own, by return through the same ways.

2. But we briefly cut short their long circuits of logical folly by acknowledging that dissolution of the body into its component parts does take place, and not only does earth, according to the Divine word, return to earth, but air and moisture also revert to the kindred element, and there takes place a return of each of our components to that nature to which it is allied; and although the human body be dispersed among carnivorous birds, or among the most savage beasts by becoming their food, and although it pass beneath the teeth of fish, and although it be changed by fire into vapour and dust, wheresoever one may in argument suppose the man to be removed, he surely remains in the world; and the world, the voice of inspiration tells us, is held by the hand of God. If thou, then, art not ignorant of any of the things in thy hand, dost thou deem the knowledge of God to be feebler than thine own power, that it should fail

to discover the most minute of the things that are within the compass of the Divine span?

XXVII. THAT IT IS POSSIBLE, WHEN THE HUMAN BODY IS DISSOLVED INTO THE ELEMENTS OF THE UNIVERSE, THAT EACH SHOULD HAVE HIS OWN BODY RESTORED FROM THE COMMON SOURCE

1. Yet it may be thou thinkest, having regard to the elements of the universe, that it is a hard thing when the air in us has been resolved into its kindred element, and the warmth, and moisture, and the earthy nature have likewise been mingled with their own kind, that from the common source there should return to the individual what belongs to itself.

2. Dost thou not then judge by human examples that even this does not surpass the limits of the Divine power? Thou hast seen surely somewhere among the habitations of men a common herd of some kind of animals collected from every quarter: yet when it is again divided among its owners, acquaintance with their homes and the marks put upon the cattle serve to restore to each his own. If thou conceivest of thyself also something like to this, thou wilt not be far from the right way: for as the soul is disposed to cling to and long for the body that has been wedded to it, there also attaches to it in secret a certain close relationship and power of recognition, in virtue of their commixture, as though some marks had been imprinted by nature, by the aid of which the community remains unconfused, separated by the distinctive signs. Now as the soul attracts again to itself that which is its own and properly belongs to it, what labour, I pray you, that is involved for the Divine power, could be a hindrance to concourse of kindred things when they are urged to their own place by the unspeakable attraction of nature, whatever it may be? For that some signs of our compound nature remain in the soul even after dissolution is shown by the dialogue in Hades , where the bodies had been conveyed to the tomb, but some bodily token still remained in the souls by which both Lazarus was recognized and the rich man was not unknown.

3. There is therefore nothing beyond probability in believing that in the bodies that rise again there will be a return from the common stock to the individual, especially for any one who examines our nature with careful attention. For neither does our being consist altogether in flux and change—for surely that which had by nature no stability would be absolutely incomprehensible—but according to the more accurate statement some one of our constituent parts is stationary while the rest goes through a process of alteration: for the body is on the one hand altered by way of growth and diminution, changing, like garments, the vesture of its successive statures, while the form, on the

other hand, remains in itself unaltered through every change, not varying from the marks once imposed upon it by nature, but appearing with its own tokens of identity in all the changes which the body undergoes.

4. We must except, however, from this statement the change which happens to the form as the result of disease: for the deformity of sickness takes possession of the form like some strange mask, and when this is removed by the word , as in the case of Naaman the Syrian, or of those whose story is recorded in the Gospel, the form that had been hidden by disease is once more by means of health restored to sight again with its own marks of identity.

5. Now to the element of our soul which is in the likeness of God it is not that which is subject to flux and change by way of alteration, but this stable and unalterable element in our composition that is allied: and since various differences of combination produce varieties of forms (and combination is nothing else than the mixture of the elements—by elements we mean those which furnish the substratum for the making of the universe, of which the human body also is composed), while the form necessarily remains in the soul as in the impression of a seal, those things which have received from the seal the impression of its stamp do not fail to be recognized by the soul, but at the time of the World-Reformation, it receives back to itself all those things which correspond to the stamp of the form: and surely all those things would so correspond which in the beginning were stamped by the form; thus it is not beyond probability that what properly belongs to the individual should once more return to it from the common source .

6. It is said also that quicksilver, if poured out from the vessel that contains it down a dusty slope, forms small globules and scatters itself over the ground, mingling with none of those bodies with which it meets: but if one should collect at one place the substance dispersed in many directions, it flows back to its kindred substance, if not hindered by anything intervening from mixing with its own kind. Something of the same sort, I think, we ought to understand also of the composite nature of man, that if only the power were given it of God, the proper parts would spontaneously unite with those belonging to them, without any obstruction on their account arising to Him Who reforms their nature.

7. Furthermore, in the case of plants that grow from the ground, we do not observe any labour on the part of nature spent on the wheat or millet or any other seed of grain or pulse, in changing it into stalk or spike or ears; for the proper nourishment passes spontaneously, without trouble, from the common source to the individuality of each of the seeds. If, then, while the moisture supplied to all the plants is common, each of those plants which is nourished

by it draws the due supply for its own growth, what new thing is it if in the doctrine of the resurrection also, as in the case of the seeds, it happens that there is an attraction on the part of each of those who rise, of what belongs to himself?

8. So that we may learn on all hands, that the preaching of the resurrection contains nothing beyond those facts which are known to us experimentally.

9. And yet we have said nothing of the most notable point concerning ourselves; I mean the first beginning of our existence. Who knows not the miracle of nature, what the maternal womb receives—what it produces? Thou seest how that which is implanted in the womb to be the beginning of the formation of the body is in a manner simple and homogeneous: but what language can express the variety of the composite body that is framed? and who, if he did not learn such a thing in nature generally, would think that to be possible which does take place—that that small thing of no account is the beginning of a thing so great? Great, I say, not only with regard to the bodily formation, but to what is more marvellous than this, I mean the soul itself, and the attributes we behold in it.

XXVIII. TO THOSE WHO SAY THAT SOULS EXISTED BEFORE BODIES, OR THAT BODIES WERE FORMED BEFORE SOULS; WHEREIN THERE IS ALSO A REFUTATION OF THE FABLES CONCERNING TRANSMIGRATION OF SOULS

1. For it is perhaps not beyond our present subject to discuss the question which has been raised in the churches touching soul and body. Some of those before our time who have dealt with the question of "principles" think it right to say that souls have a previous existence as a people in a society of their own, and that among them also there are standards of vice and of virtue, and that the soul there, which abides in goodness, remains without experience of conjunction with the body; but if it does depart from its communion with good, it falls down to this lower life, and so comes to be in a body. Others, on the contrary, marking the order of the making of man as stated by Moses, say, that the soul is second to the body in order of time, since God first took dust from the earth and formed man, and then animated the being thus formed by His breath : and by this argument they prove that the flesh is more noble than the soul; that which was previously formed than that which was afterwards infused into it: for they say that the soul was made for the body, that the thing formed might not be without breath and motion; and that everything that is made for something else is surely less precious than that for which it is made, as the Gospel tells us that "the soul is more than meat and the body than raiment ," because the latter things exist for the sake of the former—for the soul was not

made for meat nor our bodies for raiment, but when the former things were already in being the latter were provided for their needs.

2. Since then the doctrine involved in both these theories is open to criticism—the doctrine alike of those who ascribe to souls a fabulous pre-existence in a special state, and of those who think they were created at a later time than the bodies, it is perhaps necessary to leave none of the statements contained in the doctrines without examination: yet to engage and wrestle with the doctrines on each side completely, and to reveal all the absurdities involved in the theories, would need a large expenditure both of argument and of time; we shall, however, briefly survey as best we can each of the views mentioned, and then resume our subject.

3. Those who stand by the former doctrine, and assert that the state of souls is prior to their life in the flesh, do not seem to me to be clear from the fabulous doctrines of the heathen which they hold on the subject of successive incorporation: for if one should search carefully, he will find that their doctrine is of necessity brought down to this. They tell us that one of their sages said that he, being one and the same person, was born a man, and afterwards assumed the form of a woman, and flew about with the birds, and grew as a bush, and obtained the life of an aquatic creature;—and he who said these things of himself did not, so far as I can judge, go far from the truth: for such doctrines as this of saying that one soul passed through so many changes are really fitting for the chatter of frogs or jackdaws, or the stupidity of fishes, or the insensibility of trees.

4. And of such absurdity the cause is this—the supposition of the pre-existence of souls for the first principle of such doctrine leads on the argument by consequence to the next and adjacent stage, until it astonishes us by reaching this point. For if the soul, being severed from the more exalted state by some wickedness after having once, as they say, tasted corporeal life, again becomes a man, and if the life in the flesh is, as may be presumed, acknowledged to be, in comparison with the eternal and incorporeal life, more subject to passion, it naturally follows that that which comes to be in a life such as to contain more occasions of sin, is both placed in a region of greater wickedness and rendered more subject to passion than before (now passion in the human soul is a conformity to the likeness of the irrational); and that being brought into close connection with this, it descends to the brute nature: and that when it has once set out on its way through wickedness, it does not cease its advance towards evil even when found in an irrational condition: for a halt in evil is the beginning of the impulse towards virtue, and in irrational creatures virtue does not exist. Thus it will of necessity be continually changed for the worse, always

proceeding to what is more degraded and always finding out what is worse than the nature in which it is: and just as the sensible nature is lower than the rational, so too there is a descent from this to the insensible.

5. Now so far in its course their doctrine, even if it does overstep the bounds of truth, at all events derives one absurdity from another by a kind of logical sequence: but from this point onwards their teaching takes the form of incoherent fable. Strict inference points to the complete destruction of the soul; for that which has once fallen from the exalted state will be unable to halt at any measure of wickedness, but will pass by means of its relation with the passions from rational to irrational, and from the latter state will be transferred to the insensibility of plants; and on the insensible there borders, so to say, the inanimate; and on this again follows the non-existent, so that absolutely by this train of reasoning they will have the soul to pass into nothing: thus a return once more to the better state is impossible for it: and yet they make the soul return from a bush to the man: they therefore prove that the life in a bush is more precious than an incorporeal state .

6. It has been shown that the process of deterioration which takes place in the soul will probably be extended downwards; and lower than the insensible we find the inanimate, to which, by consequence, the principle of their doctrine brings the soul: but as they will not have this, they either exclude the soul from insensibility, or, if they are to bring it back to human life, they must, as has been said, declare the life of a tree to be preferable to the original state—if, that is, the fall towards vice took place from the one, and the return towards virtue takes place from the other.

7. Thus this doctrine of theirs, which maintains that souls have a life by themselves before their life in the flesh, and that they are by reason of wickedness bound to their bodies, is shown to have neither beginning nor conclusion: and as for those who assert that the soul is of later creation than the body, their absurdity was already demonstrated above .

8. The doctrine of both, then, is equally to be rejected; but I think that we ought to direct our own doctrine in the way of truth between these theories: and this doctrine is that we are not to suppose, according to the error of the heathen that the souls that revolve with the motion of the universe weighed down by some wickedness, fall to earth by inability to keep up with the swiftness of the motion of the spheres.

XXIX. AN ESTABLISHMENT OF THE DOCTRINE THAT THE CAUSE OF THE EXISTENCE OF SOUL AND BODY IS ONE AND THE SAME

1. Nor again are we in our doctrine to begin by making up man like a clay figure, and to say that the soul came into being for the sake of this; for surely in that case the intellectual nature would be shown to be less precious than the clay figure. But as man is one, the being consisting of soul and body, we are to suppose that the beginning of his existence is one, common to both parts, so that he should not be found to be antecedent and posterior to himself, if the bodily element were first in point of time, and the other were a later addition; but we are to say that in the power of God's foreknowledge (according to the doctrine laid down a little earlier in our discourse), all the fulness of human nature had pre-existence (and to this the prophetic writing bears witness, which says that God "knoweth all things before they be "), and in the creation of individuals not to place the one element before the other, neither the soul before the body, nor the contrary, that man may not be at strife against himself, by being divided by the difference in point of time.

2. For as our nature is conceived as twofold, according to the apostolic teaching, made up of the visible man and the hidden man, if the one came first and the other supervened, the power of Him that made us will be shown to be in some way imperfect, as not being completely sufficient for the whole task at once, but dividing the work, and busying itself with each of the halves in turn.

3. But just as we say that in wheat, or in any other grain, the whole form of the plant is potentially included—the leaves, the stalk, the joints, the grain, the beard—and do not say in our account of its nature that any of these things has pre-existence, or comes into being before the others, but that the power abiding in the seed is manifested in a certain natural order, not by any means that another nature is infused into it—in the same way we suppose the human germ to possess the potentiality of its nature, sown with it at the first start of its existence, and that it is unfolded and manifested by a natural sequence as it proceeds to its perfect state, not employing anything external to itself as a stepping-stone to perfection, but itself advancing its own self in due course to the perfect state; so that it is not true to say either that the soul exists before the body, or that the body exists without the soul, but that there is one beginning of both, which according to the heavenly view was laid as their foundation in the original will of God; according to the other, came into existence on the occasion of generation.

4. For as we cannot discern the articulation of the limbs in that which is implanted for the conception of the body before it begins to take form, so neither is it possible to perceive in the same the properties of the soul before

they advance to operation; and just as no one would doubt that the thing so implanted is fashioned into the different varieties of limbs and interior organs, not by the importation of any other power from without, but by the power which resides in it transforming it to this manifestation of energy,—so also we may by like reasoning equally suppose in the case of the soul that even if it is not visibly recognized by any manifestations of activity it none the less is there; for even the form of the future man is there potentially, but is concealed because it is not possible that it should be made visible before the necessary sequence of events allows it; so also the soul is there, even though it is not visible, and will be manifested by means of its own proper and natural operation, as it advances concurrently with the bodily growth.

5. For since it is not from a dead body that the potentiality for conception is secreted, but from one which is animate and alive, we hence affirm that it is reasonable that we should not suppose that what is sent forth from a living body to be the occasion of life is itself dead and inanimate; for in the flesh that which is inanimate is surely dead; and the condition of death arises by the withdrawal of the soul. Would not one therefore in this case be asserting that withdrawal is antecedent to possession—if, that is, he should maintain that the inanimate state which is the condition of death is antecedent to the soul? And if any one should seek for a still clearer evidence of the life of that particle which becomes the beginning of the living creature in its formation, it is possible to obtain an idea on this point from other signs also, by which what is animate is distinguished from what is dead. For in the case of men we consider it an evidence of life that one is warm and operative and in motion, but the chill and motionless state in the case of bodies is nothing else than deadness.

6. Since then we see that of which we are speaking to be warm and operative, we thereby draw the further inference that it is not inanimate; but as, in respect of its corporeal part, we do not say that it is flesh, and bones, and hair, and all that we observe in the human being, but that potentially it is each of these things, yet does not visibly appear to be so; so also of the part which belongs to the soul, the elements of rationality, and desire, and anger, and all the powers of the soul are not yet visible; yet we assert that they have their place in it, and that the energies of the soul also grow with the subject in a manner similar to the formation and perfection of the body.

7. For just as a man when perfectly developed has a specially marked activity of the soul, so at the beginning of his existence he shows in himself that co-operation of the soul which is suitable and conformable to his existing need, in its preparing for itself its proper dwelling-place by means of the implanted matter; for we do not suppose it possible that the soul is adapted to a strange

building, just as it is not possible that the seal impressed on wax should be fitted to an engraving that does not agree with it.

8. For as the body proceeds from a very small original to the perfect state, so also the operation of the soul, growing in correspondence with the subject, gains and increases with it. For at its first formation there comes first of all its power of growth and nutriment alone, as though it were some root buried in the ground; for the limited nature of the recipient does not admit of more; then, as the plant comes forth to the light and shows its shoot to the sun, the gift of sensibility blossoms in addition, but when at last it is ripened and has grown up to its proper height, the power of reason begins to shine forth like a fruit, not appearing in its whole vigour all at once, but by care increasing with the perfection of the instrument, bearing always as much fruit as the powers of the subject allow.

9. If, however, thou seekest to trace the operation of the soul in the formation of the body, "take heed to thyself," as Moses says, and thou wilt read, as in a book, the history of the works of the soul; for nature itself expounds to thee, more clearly than any discourse, the varied occupations of the soul in the body, alike in general and in particular acts of construction.

10. But I deem it superfluous to declare at length in words what is to be found in ourselves, as though we were expounding some wonder that lay beyond our boundaries:—who that looks on himself needs words to teach him his own nature? For it is possible for one who considers the mode of his own life, and learns how closely concerned the body is in every vital operation, to know in what the vegetative principle of the soul was occupied on the occasion of the first formation of that which was beginning its existence; so that hereby also it is clear to those who have given any attention to the matter, that the thing which was implanted by separation from the living body for the production of the living being was not a thing dead or inanimate in the laboratory of nature.

11. Moreover we plant in the ground the kernels of fruits, and portions torn from roots, not deprived by death of the vital power which naturally resides in them, but preserving in themselves, hidden indeed, yet surely living, the property of their prototype; the earth that surrounds them does not implant such a power from without, infusing it from itself (for surely then even dead wood would proceed to growth), but it makes that manifest which resides in them, nourishing it by its own moisture, perfecting the plant into root, and bark, and pith, and shoots of branches, which could not happen were not a natural power implanted with it, which drawing to itself from its surroundings

its kindred and proper nourishment, becomes a bush, or a tree, or an ear of grain, or some plant of the class of shrubs.

XXX. A BRIEF EXAMINATION OF THE CONSTRUCTION OF OUR BODIES FROM A MEDICAL POINT OF VIEW

1. Now the exact structure of our body each man teaches himself by his experiences of sight and light and perception, having his own nature to instruct him; any one too may learn everything accurately who takes up the researches which those skilled in such matters have worked out in books. And of these writers some learnt by dissection the position of our individual organs; others also considered and expounded the reason for the existence of all the parts of the body; so that the knowledge of the human frame which hence results is sufficient for students. But if any one further seeks that the Church should be his teacher on all these points, so that he may not need for anything the voice of those without (for this is the wont of the spiritual sheep, as the Lord says, that they hear not a strange voice), we shall briefly take in hand the account of these matters also.

2. We note concerning our bodily nature three things, for the sake of which our particular parts were formed. Life is the cause of some, good life of others, others again are adapted with a view to the succession of descendants. All things in us which are of such a kind that without them it is not possible that human life should exist, we consider as being in three parts; in the brain, the heart, and the liver. Again, all that are a sort of additional blessings, nature's liberality, whereby she bestows on man the gift of living well, are the organs of sense; for such things do not constitute our life, since even where some of them are wanting man is often none the less in a condition of life; but without these forms of activity it is impossible to enjoy participation in the pleasures of life. The third aim regards the future, and the succession of life. There are also certain other organs besides these, which help, in common with all the others, to subserve the continuance of life, importing by their own means the proper supplies, as the stomach and the lungs, the latter fanning by respiration the fire at the heart, the former introducing the nourishment for the internal organs.

3. Our structure, then, being thus divided, we have carefully to mark that our faculty for life is not supported in any one way by some single organ, but nature, while distributing the means for our existence among several parts, makes the contribution of each individual necessary for the whole; just as the things which nature contrives for the security and beauty of life are also numerous, and differ much among themselves.

4. We ought, however, I think, first to discuss briefly the first beginnings of the things which contribute to the constitution of our life. As for the material of the whole body which serves as a common substratum for the particular members, it may for the present be left without remark; for a discussion as to natural substance in general will not be of any assistance to our purpose with regard to the consideration of the parts.

5. As it is then acknowledged by all that there is in us a share of all that we behold as elements in the universe—of heat and cold, and of the other pair of qualities of moisture and dryness—we must discuss them severally.

6. We see then that the powers which control life are three, of which the first by its heat produces general warmth, the second by its moisture keeps damp that which is warmed, so that the living being is kept in an intermediate condition by the equal balance of the forces exerted by the quality of each of the opposing natures (the moist element not being dried up by excess of heat, nor the hot element quenched by the prevalence of moisture); and the third power by its own agency holds together the separate members in a certain agreement and harmony, connecting them by the ties which it itself furnishes, and sending into them all that self-moving and determining force, on the failure of which the member becomes relaxed and deadened, being left destitute of the determining spirit.

7. Or rather, before dealing with these, it is right that we should mark the skilled workmanship of nature in the actual construction of the body. For as that which is hard and resistent does not admit the action of the senses (as we may see in the instance of our own bones, and in that of plants in the ground, where we remark indeed a certain form of life in that they grow and receive nourishment, yet the resistent character of their substance does not allow them sensation), for this reason it was necessary that some wax-like formation, so to say, should be supplied for the action of the senses, with the faculty of being impressed with the stamp of things capable of striking them, neither becoming confused by excess of moisture (for the impress would not remain in moist substance), nor resisting by extraordinary solidity (for that which is unyielding would not receive any mark from the impressions), but being in a state between softness and hardness, in order that the living being might not be destitute of the fairest of all the operations of nature—I mean the motion of sense.

8. Now as a soft and yielding substance, if it had no assistance from the hard parts, would certainly have, like molluscs, neither motion nor articulation, nature accordingly mingles in the body the hardness of the bones, and uniting these by close connection one to another, and knitting their joints together by means of the sinews, thus plants around them the flesh which

receives sensations, furnished with a somewhat harder and more highly-strung surface than it would otherwise have had.

9. While resting, then, the whole weight of the body on this substance of the bones, as on some columns that carry a mass of building, she did not implant the bone undivided through the whole structure: for in that case man would have remained without motion or activity, if he had been so constructed, just like a tree that stands on one spot without either the alternate motion of legs to advance its motion or the service of hands to minister to the conveniences of life: but now we see that she contrived that the instrument should be rendered capable of walking and working by this device, after she had implanted in the body, by the determining spirit which extends through the nerves, the impulse and power for motion. And hence is produced the service of the hands, so varied and multiform, and answering to every thought. Hence are produced, as though by some mechanical contrivance, the turnings of the neck, and the bending and raising of the head, and the action of the chin, and the separation of the eyelids, that takes place with a thought, and the movements of the other joints, by the tightening or relaxation of certain nerves. And the power that extends through these exhibits a sort of independent impulse, working with the spirit of its will by a sort of natural management, in each particular part; but the root of all, and the principle of the motions of the nerves, is found in the nervous tissue that surrounds the brain.

10. We consider, then, that we need not spend more time in inquiring in which of the vital members such a thing resides, when the energy of motion is shown to be here. But that the brain contributes to life in a special degree is shown clearly by the result of the opposite conditions: for if the tissue surrounding it receives any wound or lesion, death immediately follows the injury, nature being unable to endure the hurt even for a moment; just as, when a foundation is withdrawn, the whole building collapses with the part; and that member, from an injury to which the destruction of the whole living being clearly follows, may properly be acknowledged to contain the cause of life.

11. But as furthermore in those who have ceased to live, when the heat that is implanted in our nature is quenched, that which has become dead grows cold, we hence recognize the vital cause also in heat: for we must of necessity acknowledge that the living being subsists by the presence of that, which failing, the condition of death supervenes. And of such a force we understand the heart to be as it were the fountain-head and principle, as from it pipe-like passages, growing one from another in many ramifications, diffuse in the whole body the warm and fiery spirit.

12. And since some nourishment must needs also be provided by nature for the element of heat—for it is not possible that the fire should last by itself, without being nourished by its proper food—therefore the channels of the blood, issuing from the liver as from a fountainhead, accompany the warm spirit everywhere in its way throughout the body, that the one may not by isolation from the other become a disease and destroy the constitution. Let this instruct those who go beyond the bounds of fairness, as they learn from nature that covetousness is a disease that breeds destruction.

13. But since the Divinity alone is free from needs, while human poverty requires external aid for its own subsistence, nature therefore, in addition to those three powers by which we said that the whole body is regulated, brings in imported matter from without, introducing by different entrances that which is suitable to those powers.

14. For to the fount of the blood, which is the liver, she furnishes its supply by food: for that which from time to time is imported in this way prepares the springs of blood to issue from the liver, as the snow on the mountain by its own moisture increases the springs in the low ground, forcing its own fluid deep down to the veins below.

15. The breath in the heart is supplied by means of the neighbouring organ, which is called the lungs, and is a receptacle for air, drawing the breath from without through the windpipe inserted in it, which extends to the mouth. The heart being placed in the midst of this organ (and itself also moving incessantly in imitation of the action of the ever-moving fire), draws to itself, somewhat as the bellows do in the forges, a supply from the adjacent air, filling its recesses by dilatation, and while it fans its own fiery element, breathes upon the adjoining tubes; and this it does not cease to do, drawing the external air into its own recesses by dilatation, and by compression infusing the air from itself into the tubes.

16. And this seems to me to be the cause of this spontaneous respiration of ours; for often the mind is occupied in discourse with others, or is entirely quiescent when the body is relaxed in sleep, but the respiration of air does not cease, though the will gives no co-operation to this end. Now I suppose, since the heart is surrounded by the lungs, and in the back part of its own structure is attached to them, moving that organ by its own dilatations and compressions, that the inhaling and exhaling of the air is brought about by the lungs: for as they are a lightly built and porous body, and have all their recesses opening at the base of the windpipe, when they contract and are compressed they necessarily force out by pressure the air that is left in their cavities; and,

when they expand and open, draw the air, by their distention, into the void by suction.

17. This then is the cause of this involuntary respiration—the impossibility that the fiery element should remain at rest: for as the operation of motion is proper to heat, and we understand that the principle of heat is to be found in the heart, the continual motion going on in this organ produces the incessant inspiration and exhalation of the air through the lungs: wherefore also when the fiery element is unnaturally augmented, the breathing of those fevered subjects becomes more rapid, as though the heart were endeavouring to quench the flame implanted in it by more violent breathing.

18. But since our nature is poor and in need of supplies for its own maintenance from all quarters, it not only lacks air of its own, and the breath which excites heat, which it imports from without for the preservation of the living being, but the nourishment it finds to fill out the proportions of the body is an importation. Accordingly, it supplies the deficiency by food and drink, implanting in the body a certain faculty for appropriating that which it requires, and rejecting that which is superfluous, and for this purpose too the fire of the heart gives nature no small assistance.

19. For since, according to the account we have given, the heart which kindles by its warm breath the individual parts, is the most important of the vital organs, our Maker caused it to be operative with its efficacious power at all points, that no part of it might be left ineffectual or unprofitable for the regulation of the whole organism. Behind, therefore, it enters the lungs, and, by its continuous motion, drawing that organ to itself, it expands the passages to inhale the air, and compressing them again it brings about the exspiration of the imprisoned air; while in front, attached to the space at the upper extremity of the stomach, it warms it and makes it respond by motion to its own activity, rousing it, not to inhale air, but to receive its appropriate food: for the entrances for breath and food are near one another, extending lengthwise one alongside the other, and are terminated in their upper extremity by the same boundary, so that their mouths are contiguous and the passages come to an end together in one mouth, from which the entrance of food is effected through the one, and that of the breath through the other.

20. Internally, however, the closeness of the connection of the passages is not maintained throughout; for the heart intervening between the base of the two, infuses in the one the powers for respiration, and in the other for nutriment. Now the fiery element is naturally inclined to seek for the material which serves as fuel, and this necessarily happens with regard to the receptacle of nourishment; for the more it becomes penetrated by fire through the neigh-

bouring warmth, the more it draws to itself what nourishes the heat. And this sort of impulse we call appetite.

21. But if the organ which contains the food should obtain sufficient material, not even so does the activity of the fire become quiescent: but it produces a sort of melting of the material just as in a foundry, and, dissolving the solids, pours them out and transfers them, as it were from a funnel, to the neighbouring passages: then separating the coarser from the pure substance, it passes the fine part through certain channels to the entrance of the liver, and expels the sedimentary matter of the food to the wider passages of the bowels, and by turning it over in their manifold windings retains the food for a time in the intestines, lest if it were easily got rid of by a straight passage it might at once excite the animal again to appetite, and man, like the race of irrational animals, might never cease from this sort of occupation.

22. As we saw, however, that the liver has especial need of the co-operation of heat for the conversion of the fluids into blood, while this organ is in position distant from the heart (for it would, I imagine, have been impossible that, being one principle or root of the vital power, it should not be hampered by vicinity with another such principle), in order that the system may suffer no injury by the distance at which the heat-giving substance is placed, a muscular passage (and this, by those skilled in such matters, is called the artery) receives the heated air from the heart and conveys it to the liver, making its opening there somewhere beside the point at which the fluids enter, and, as it warms the moist substance by its heat, blends with the liquid something akin to fire, and makes the blood appear red with the fiery tint it produces.

23. Issuing thence again, certain twin channels, each enclosing its own current like a pipe, disperse air and blood (that the liquid substance may have free course when accompanied and lightened by the motion of the heated substance) in divers directions over the whole body, breaking at every part into countless branching channels; while as the two principles of the vital powers mingle together (that alike which disperses heat, and that which supplies moisture to all parts of the body), they make, as it were, a sort of compulsory contribution from the substance with which they deal to the supreme force in the vital economy.

24. Now this force is that which is considered as residing in the cerebral membranes and the brain, from which it comes that every movement of a joint, every contraction of the muscles, every spontaneous influence that is exerted upon the individual members, renders our earthen statue active and mobile as though by some mechanism. For the most pure form of heat and the most subtle form of liquid, being united by their respective forces through a

process of mixture and combination, nourish and sustain by their moisture the brain, and hence in turn, being rarefied to the most pure condition, the exhalation that proceeds from that organ anoints the membrane which encloses the brain, which, reaching from above downwards like a pipe, extending through the successive vertebrae, is (itself and the marrow which is contained in it) conterminous with the base of the spine, itself giving like a charioteer the impulse and power to all the meeting-points of bones and joints, and to the branches of the muscles, for the motion or rest of the particular parts.

25. For this cause too it seems to me that it has been granted a more secure defence, being distinguished, in the head, by a double shelter of bones round about, and in the vertebrae of the neck by the bulwarks formed by the projections of the spine as well as by the diversified interlacings of the very form of those vertebrae, by which it is kept in freedom from all harm, enjoying safety by the defence that surrounds it.

26. So too one might suppose of the heart, that it is itself like some safe house fitted with the most solid defences, fortified by the enclosing walls of the bones round about; for in rear there is the spine, strengthened on either side by the shoulder-blades, and on each flank the enfolding position of the ribs makes that which is in the midst between them difficult to injure; while in front the breast-bone and the juncture of the collar-bone serve as a defence, that its safety may be guarded at all points from external causes of danger.

27. As we see in husbandry, when the rain fall from the clouds or the overflow from the river channels causes the land beneath it to be saturated with moisture (let us suppose for our argument a garden, nourishing within its own compass countless varieties of trees, and all the forms of plants that grow from the ground, and whereof we contemplate the figure, quality, and individuality in great variety of detail); then, as these are nourished by the liquid element while they are in one spot, the power which supplies moisture to each individual among them is one in nature; but the individuality of the plants so nourished changes the liquid element into different qualities; for the same substance becomes bitter in wormwood, and is changed into a deadly juice in hemlock, and becomes different in different other plants, in saffron, in balsam, in the poppy: for in one it becomes hot, in another cold, in another it obtains the middle quality: and in laurel and mastick it is scented, and in the fig and the pear it is sweetened, and by passing through the vine it is turned into the grape and into wine; while the juice of the apple, the redness of the rose, the radiance of the lily, the blue of the violet, the purple of the hyacinthine dye, and all that we behold in the earth, arise from one and the same moisture, and are separated into so many varieties in respect of figure and aspect and quality; the same

sort of wonder is wrought in the animated soil of our being by Nature, or rather by Nature's Lord. Bones, cartilages, veins, arteries, nerves, ligatures, flesh, skin, fat, hair, glands, nails, eyes, nostrils, ears,—all such things as these, and countless others in addition, while separated from one another by various peculiarities, are nourished by the one form of nourishment in ways proper to their own nature, in the sense that the nourishment, when it is brought into close relation with any of the subjects, is also changed according to that to which it approaches, and becomes adapted and allied to the special nature of the part. For if it should be in the neighbourhood of the eye, it blends with the visual part and is appropriately distributed by the difference of the coats round the eye, among the single parts; or, if it flow to the auditory parts, it is mingled with the auscultatory nature, or if it is in the lip, it becomes lip; and it grows solid in bone, and grows soft in marrow, and is made tense with the sinew, and extended with the surface, and passes into the nails, and is fined down for the growth of the hair, by correspondent exhalations, producing hair that is somewhat curly or wavy if it makes its way through winding passages, while, if the course of the exhalations that go to form the hair lies straight, it renders the hair stiff and straight.

28. Our argument, however, has wandered far from its purpose, going deep into the works of nature, and endeavouring to describe how and from what materials our particular organs are formed, those, I mean, intended for life and for good life, and any other class which we included with these in our first division.

29. For our purpose was to show that the seminal cause of our constitution is neither a soul without body, nor a body without soul, but that, from animated and living bodies, it is generated at the first as a living and animate being, and that our humanity takes it and cherishes it like a nursling with the resources she herself possesses, and it thus grows on both sides and makes its growth manifest correspondingly in either part:—for it at once displays, by this artificial and scientific process of formation, the power of soul that is interwoven in it, appearing at first somewhat obscurely, but afterwards increasing in radiance concurrently with the perfecting of the work.

30. And as we may see with stone-carvers—for the artist's purpose is to produce in stone the figure of some animal; and with this in his mind, he first severs the stone from its kindred matter, and then, by chipping away the superfluous parts of it, advances somehow by the intermediate step of his first outline to the imitation which he has in his purpose, so that even an unskilled observer may, by what he sees, conjecture the aim of his art; again, by working at it, he brings it more nearly to the semblance of the object he has in view;

lastly, producing in the material the perfect and finished figure, he brings his art to its conclusion, and that which a little before was a shapeless stone is a lion, or a man, or whatsoever it may be that the artist has made, not by the change of the material into the figure, but by the figure being wrought upon the material. If one supposes the like in the case of the soul he is not far from probability; for we say that Nature, the all-contriving, takes from its kindred matter the part that comes from the man, and moulds her statue within herself. And as the form follows upon the gradual working of the stone, at first somewhat indistinct, but more perfect after the completion of the work, so too in the moulding of its instrument the form of the soul is expressed in the substratum, incompletely in that which is still incomplete, perfect in that which is perfect; indeed it would have been perfect from the beginning had our nature not been maimed by evil. Thus our community in that generation which is subject to passion and of animal nature, brings it about that the Divine image does not at once shine forth at our formation, but brings man to perfection by a certain method and sequence, through those attributes of the soul which are material, and belong rather to the animal creation.

31. Some such doctrine as this the great apostle also teaches us in his Epistle to the Corinthians, when he says, "When I was a child, I spake as a child, I understood as a child, I thought as a child; but when I became a man I put away childish things "; not that the soul which arises in the man is different from that which we know to be in the boy, and the childish intellect fails while the manly intellect takes its being in us; but that the same soul displays its imperfect condition in the one, its perfect state in the other.

32. For we say that those things are alive which spring up and grow, and no one would deny that all things that participate in life and natural motion are animate, yet at the same time one cannot say that such life partakes of a perfect soul,—for though a certain animate operation exists in plants, it does not attain to the motions of sense; and on the other hand, though a certain further animate power exists in the brutes, neither does this attain perfection, since it does not contain in itself the grace of reason and intelligence.

33. And even so we say that the true and perfect soul is the human soul, recognized by every operation; and anything else that shares in life we call animate by a sort of customary misuse of language, because in these cases the soul does not exist in a perfect condition, but only certain parts of the operation of the soul, which in man also (according to Moses' mystical account of man's origin) we learn to have accrued when he made himself like this sensuous world. Thus Paul, advising those who were able to hear him to lay hold on perfection, indicates also the mode in which they may attain that object, telling

them that they must "put off the old man," and put on the man "which is renewed after the image of Him that created him ."

34. Now may we all return to that Divine grace in which God at the first created man, when He said, "Let us make man in our image and likeness"; to Whom be glory and might for ever and ever. Amen.

Printed in Great Britain
by Amazon

21680517R00047